Internships, High-Impact Practices, and Provocative Praxis in Higher Education

This authored text critically examines the theory and practice of college internship programs grounded in equity, diversity, inclusion, and access (EDIA) to examine issues such as infrastructure, inclusion, and privilege through "provocative praxis," a form of provocative inquiry that drives the ethics of pedagogy to envision student success both equitably and sustainably. Chapters use real-life, scenario-based examples through a social-justice framework to engage readers and spark multi-directional discussion aimed at removing obstacles to equitable participation in internships for all students. Ultimately, this book offers a holistic understanding of internships that factors in the social, economic, and cultural challenges faced by college students today, and calls for wholescale reform to college campus internship programs.

Beth Manke is Professor of Human Development and Senior Faculty Fellow with the Academic Internships Office, Center for Community Engagement, California State University, Long Beach, USA.

Bonnie Gasior is Professor of Spanish, California State University, Long Beach and Faculty Fellow with the Institute of Teaching & Learning, Chancellor's Office, California State University, USA.

Michelle Chang is Director of the Academic Internships Office, Center for Community Engagement, California State University, Long Beach, USA.

Routledge Research in Higher Education

Universities in Times of Crisis and Disruption
Dislocated Complexity
Lorraine Ling and Kay Livingston

Developing a Model for Culturally Responsive Experiential Education
Teachers as Allies in Student Journeys of Decolonization
Elizabeth Laura Hope Yomantas

Creating Supportive Spaces for Pregnant and Parenting College Students
Contemporary Understandings of Title IX
Edited by Catherine L. Riley and Katie B. Garner

Gamification and Design Thinking in Higher Education
Case Studies for Instructional Innovation in the Economics Classroom
Carmen Bueno Muñoz, Núria Hernández Nanclares, Luis R. Murillo Zamorano, and José Ángel López Sánchez

The Development of Professional Identity in Higher Education
Continuing and Advancing Professionalism
Edited by Myint Swe Khine and Abdulghani Muthanna

Internships, High-Impact Practices, and Provocative Praxis in Higher Education
A Social Justice Framework Based on Equity, Diversity, Inclusion, and Access
Beth Manke, Bonnie Gasior, and Michelle Chang

For more information about this series, please visit: www.routledge.com/Routledge-Research-in-Higher-Education/book-series/RRHE

Internships, High-Impact Practices, and Provocative Praxis in Higher Education

A Social Justice Framework Based on Equity, Diversity, Inclusion, and Access

Authored by Beth Manke, Bonnie Gasior and Michelle Chang

NEW YORK AND LONDON

First published 2024
by Routledge
605 Third Avenue, New York, NY 10158

and by Routledge
4 Park Square, Milton Park, Abingdon, Oxon, OX14 4RN

Routledge is an imprint of the Taylor & Francis Group, an informa business

© 2024 Beth Manke, Bonnie Gasior and Michelle Chang

The right of Beth Manke, Bonnie Gasior and Michelle Chang to be identified as authors of this work has been asserted in accordance with sections 77 and 78 of the Copyright, Designs and Patents Act 1988.

All rights reserved. No part of this book may be reprinted or reproduced or utilised in any form or by any electronic, mechanical, or other means, now known or hereafter invented, including photocopying and recording, or in any information storage or retrieval system, without permission in writing from the publishers.

Trademark notice: Product or corporate names may be trademarks or registered trademarks, and are used only for identification and explanation without intent to infringe.

ISBN: 9781032283326 (hbk)
ISBN: 9781032716022 (pbk)
ISBN: 9781003296324 (ebk)

DOI: 10.4324/9781003296324

Typeset in Times New Roman
by Apex CoVantage, LLC

We dedicate this book to the thousands of student interns we have worked with in and beyond the classroom over the past twenty-plus years, especially our Students of Color, whose endeavors inform the contours of this book.

Contents

	Preface	*viii*
	Acknowledgments	*xii*
1	HIPs in Hindsight, HIPS in Foresight: A Social-Justice Reimagining of Internships in the 21st Century	1
2	Institutional Infrastructure: Centralization, Workload, Collaboration & Funding	18
3	Intersequity, Students of Color, and the Perils of Unpaid Internships	40
4	Community Partners as Critical Coefficients in the Internship Equation	62
5	Assessment as a Catalyst for Addressing Equity in Internships	89
	Afterword: Beyond InternsHIPs	*106*
	Index	*109*

Preface

Beth (Manke) has often stated in the last year and a half, either when responding to others' queries about the genesis of *InternsHIPs* or when reminding Michelle and Bonnie about workplace serendipity, "Coincidence made us colleagues, but our shared passion and commitment to equitable access to and participation in internships made us co-authors." Indeed, the impetus for this book evolved from our common interests in internships and related opportunities we seized. What ultimately gave it shape and form, however, and perhaps ironically, were the challenges we faced in each of our roles on campus.

In fleshing out those challenges, frustrations cathartically turned to fodder. Whether at a brick-and-mortar meeting or in a Zoom room, we found ourselves revisiting the same thorny internship questions—*How do we ensure equitable access to internship opportunities? Why doesn't our campus invest in and resource these transformative learning experiences? How do we elevate student and site host voices in a way that attests to the power of mentorship?* Faced with a paucity of clear answers and rather than shrug our shoulders, we dug in our heels. Our speculation deepened as we began talking to and interviewing other professionals, many of whom requested anonymity, across the country about their own college internship programs. The moments of epiphany, at once stunning and validating, confirmed that many others were, in fact, grappling with the same issues and, as such, could benefit from our collective work to implement equitable internship opportunities and our commitment to confronting, complicating, and nuancing these critical conversations.

To begin, we would be remiss in overlooking the trailblazing scholars who have written about internships for years, if not decades, some of whom have dedicated their entire careers to them. Indeed, this book is indebted to and informed by their scholarship. What *InternsHIPs* does differently, though, is that it looks at EDIA *holistically*. While our colleagues tackle specific internship issues in their own research or on particular campuses, *InternsHIPs* situates the spectrum around the EDIA table to impel restless and unrelenting dialogue. Similarly, our book approaches these student-centered issues from a leadership perspective, arguing that an internship program is only as good as the support, both material and symbolic, it receives from campus administrators.

Our hope is that in this way, internship champions will be inspired to engage in internship discussions on their own campuses vis-à-vis a term we explain more fully in the introduction—provocative praxis. Provocative praxis is the antithesis of prescription; it involves asking uncomfortable questions that lead to more (uncomfortable) questions before arriving at contextually specific answers. Not only do we engage in provocative praxis throughout this book as it applies to the internship issues we broach, but we also engaged in our own sort of provocative praxis with one another during the writing process. In order to authentically advance our agenda, we pushed ourselves, each other, and the envelope to consider new ways of thinking. Additionally, the case studies culled and peppered throughout the chapters exemplify our ideas and attest to the endemic nature of myriad college internship issues. Content-wise, they originate from across the United States and internationally, including our own campus, a public research university and the second largest in the 23-campus California State University system, which qualifies as both a Hispanic and an Asian American and Native American Pacific Islander (AANAPI)-serving institution. It should come as no surprise that over half of our student body identifies as first-generation and/or low-income. Much of what we write about, then, is gleaned from and legitimized by first-hand knowledge. Because each of us brought disparate yet unique, complementary perspectives to the project—Beth's extensive work on campus to institutionalize internships, Michelle's work in career services and efforts as the Internship Specialist in California State University, Long Beach's second largest college, Bonnie's experience with other HIPs and other discipline-specific publishing endeavors—we assigned chapter leads based on our intellectual and practical strengths and coupled the strategy with extensive co-editing to project a consistent voice.

Our appreciation for and experience with EDIA manifests broadly, such as participation in campus Intergroup Dialogue as well as leading high-impact-oriented programs, such as University Honors, where we interrogated our own roles in complex systems of racial inequity as they relate to HIPs. Ancillary endeavors include multi-year leadership programs, where we were trained to identify and deploy various leadership frames as we led campus-wide initiatives like the crafting of internship programs; Design Your Life training at the Stanford University Design School, where we helped re-design materials to make them more culturally sensitive; attending the AACU Institute on High Impact Practices and Student Success, where we developed a comprehensive action plan to establish institutional infrastructure on our campus to support access to participation in internships for all students; and efforts to address the student mental health epidemic, with the idea that student wellness is a foundational component of student success.

Lawrence R. Samuel (2018) psychologically ponders the question "Why do Writers Write?" and answers by summarizing insights from Kelly Cherry in her article, "Beginning" (1995):

> Writers are driven by a primal urge to tell people who they are. Readers necessarily have some sense of the identity of the writer whose work they choose to peruse, lending an existential dimension to the endeavor. Writing is thus a means of becoming more human.
>
> (para. 1)

Considering that this applies more to commercial writers, we gladly provide some biographical information for our readers in the spirit of transparency and in anticipation of imminent Google searches.

In his novel *Shadow of the Wind* (2001), Spanish author Carlos Ruiz Zafón comments on the connection between what we read and ourselves: "Books are mirrors: you only see in them what you already have inside you" (p. 34). Just as readers invariably bring subjectivity to the reading experience, authors similarly angle their own mirrors upon the writing process. Our positionalities as EDIA "authorities"—as well as any privilege those positions confer—warrant addressing. Two of us—Beth Manke and Bonnie Gasior—identify as white women, while Michelle Chang identifies as Taiwanese-American and as a Person of Color. We understand, therefore, that some readers may question our collective legitimacy as equity theoreticians. Although we agree that these critical conversations are most accepted and authentic when they originate with those who have experienced racial inequity—as Michelle has—our collective intersectionality underscores our own equity battles that originate from the markers of gender and socioeconomics. This lived experience between the three of us, at the very least, elevates our sensitivity to critical perspectives on racial equity. As a result, we stand behind our contributions to EDIA conversations as intersectional women who further benefit from the wisdom of our sole Person of Color co-author.

When A. A. Bergerson (2003) asks "Is there room for [W]hite scholars in fighting racism in education?," Lori D. Patton and Chayla Haynes (2020), two Women of Color, answer optimistically: "Absolutely. Not only is there room to fight racism, but also to dismantle it. Reimagining Whiteness requires seeing yourself as fully capable of responding to racial inequity and engaging other White people in this process as a non-negotiable imperative" (p. 42). They further reassure non-Persons of Color that, "It's okay to be White. White people can make valuable contributions to shift the course of racial equity" (p. 43). Indeed, *InternsHIPs* substantiates that Persons of Color and non-Persons of Color can and should work together to carry out this important, social-justice work. Ultimately, our self-disclosures have helped us (and will hopefully help others!) to overcome the fear of mistake-making that often paralyzes non-Persons of Color to instead spark institutional activism and change. With their claims in mind, we hope the readers of this manuscript enjoy manifold moments of meaningful self-recognition, glean from them what brought us as scholars to this endeavor, and appreciate why both matter in the context of a book grounded in EDIA.

In her latest California State University, Long Beach "Provost's Message" (2023, July), Karen Scissum Gunn throws down the gauntlet of student success, which, although written in an Academic Affairs context, applies to anyone working in a student-adjacent position at any university:

> Let's ask ourselves: how do I ensure that I am leading, teaching, and learning with compassion and justice at the center? How can I find ways to remove barriers for ALL those around me? What challenges may others be facing, both visible and invisible? Higher education is at a critical moment, but it is my hope we can ALL renew our commitment to our purpose as The Beach. Each of us possesses a power to transform lives around us. It starts with us.
>
> (para. 3–4)

It is in this spirit of shared responsibility that we hope galvanizes our readers (provocatively) to think about their own internship programs—both the opportunities and the challenges—in novel ways that, as a result, strive to level the internship landscape for the twenty-first century students.

References

Bergerson, A. A. (2003). Critical race theory and white racism: Is there room for white scholars in fighting racism in education? *International Journal of Qualitative Studies in Education*, *16*(1), 51–63. https://doi.org/10.1080/0951839032000033527

Cherry, K. (1995, November). Beginning. *Writer*, 22.

Patton, L. D., & Haynes, C. (2020). Dear white people: Reimagining whiteness in the struggle for racial equity. *Change: The Magazine of Higher Learning*, *52*(2), 41–45. https://doi.org/10.1080/00091383.2020.1732775

Ruiz Zafón, C. (2001). *Shadow of the wind* (L. Graves, Trans.). Penguin Books.

Samuel, L. R. (2018, February 13). Why do writers write? *Psychology Today*. https://www.psychologytoday.com/us/blog/psychology-yesterday/201802/why-do-writers-write

Scissum Gunn, K. (2023, July). *Provost's Message*. California State University. csulb.edu

Acknowledgments

B. M.: I am grateful to several people who made this book possible. First, and foremost, my husband Omer Miller, who is a consistent source of support, both emotional and instrumental. He took on most of our household tasks over the past year giving me the gift of time to write. He also listened when I needed to vent, encouraged me when I had writer's block, and made me laugh every day. A special thanks to my friends and collaborators on this book, Bonnie Gasior and Michelle Chang. Bonnie's experience with the publishing process and her brilliant mind kept us focused and on schedule while Michelle's real-world expertise in internship programming kept us grounded.

I would also like to thank my mother Gale Manke, a retired professor of nursing, for modeling what equity and inclusion in higher education should look like during a time when EDIA was not yet a priority for campuses. Thanks to my nephews Spencer Lee and Trevor Lee who as college students helped me see that that my true calling was as a faculty advocate for students and equitable internship opportunities.

And finally, I am indebted to my colleagues who have partnered with me over the years to launch internship programs and research projects from which the content of this book is drawn (e.g., the Long Beach Community Internship Program, College Corps@the Beach, HIPs@the Beach, etc.): Juan Benitez, Jane Conoley, Kim Kelly, Kristal King, Kerry Klima, Claudia Lopez, Sarah Monteiro, Amy Rasmussen, Lizzet Rojas, Karyn Scissum Gunn, Lisa Sparks, Kaitlyn Stormes, Brian Trimble, Catherine Ward, Jeff Williams, Christine Whitcraft, Jake Wilson, and Kelly Young.

B. G.: Several individuals deserve special thanks for their support over the last year and a half: My husband, Tim Rosenow, who never once questioned my decision to forgo a social event or a TV series in favor of working on this book, often opting instead to accompany me in writing solidarity; Beth Manke—leader, colleague, friend, partner in crime, and now, collaborator—who brought insight, wit, and levity to the writing process (and life in general); Darci Strother—amiga, MHFA confidant, and go-to sounding board—for her listening, noticing, and validation skills. ALGEE would be proud; Michelle Chang, for educating me on myriad practical internship matters; you truly embody the position "internship specialist"; Alexis Pavenick, librarian extraordinaire, who was always available for reference questions and moral support (if not a bottle of wine); and to the little humans in my life, my nieces, Olivia and Alaina, and nephew, Cameron, whose privileged lives make me feel grateful as an aunt yet conflicted as a scholar. I hope someday they read this book and are inspired to make their own EDIA contributions to the world!

I would also like to thank the following friends and colleagues who made it a point to check in or cheer from the sidelines: Courtney Ahrens, Mindy Badía, Lori Bernard, Alyson Kavalukas, Laura Duvall, Carol Dzadony-Mancini, Jennifer Fleming, Yolanda Gamboa, Charles Ganelin, Christine Jocoy, Marie Kelleher, Melissa Lyon, Mark Malek, Irene Malek, Tomas Mielke, Markus Muller, Brad Nelson, Kristin Rosenow, Alaine O'Campo, Sonia Pérez-Villanueva, Amy Peters, Max Rosenkrantz, and Kamara Ya.

Lastly, I am grateful to the 2021 CLA Sabbatical Committee at CSULB, who selected my application for a one-semester research leave in spring 2022, which allowed for progress on two draft chapters.

M. C.: I never imagined writing a book, and when Beth and Bonnie invited me to join them in this endeavor, I had my doubts—am I smart or experienced enough to contribute anything to this manuscript? They validated my experiences and encouraged me throughout this process. So, first, I would like to thank my colleagues, mentors, and co-collaborators: Beth Manke, for being my biggest champion, challenging me to think creatively, and role modeling what it means to lead with empathy; and Bonnie Gasior, for your guidance in the writing process and being an example of what it means to be student-centered. Thank you for believing in my abilities (especially when I did not) and for continuing to challenge and support me.

To my wonderful husband, Saroeuth Chim, thank you for being an amazing partner. Having a toddler and writing a book meant many missed bedtimes and I would not have been able to do this without you. And to my daughter Lillian, you have brought us so much joy (and sleepless nights), may you reap the benefits of this work and may your journey be filled with adventure, growth, and love!

I want to thank my parents, Bill and Joan Chang, for always emphasizing the importance of hard work and dedication. Without that foundation, I would not be where I am today. They uprooted their lives, immigrated to a new country, and worked so hard so that I could have every opportunity to succeed. I am so proud to be your daughter.

Lastly, to my colleagues, co-conspirators, and friends: Amy Rasmussen, Barbara Kim, May Lin, Jolene McCall, Elizabeth Lim, Sarah Nguyen, and Nichelle Buck—I am so grateful for your collaboration and friendship!

Collectively, we are grateful to our internship partners and organizations, who collaborated with us to do the work of prototyping equitable internship practices, mentoring student interns, and ensuring high-quality internship experiences. Indeed, you remind us, as per the African proverb that "it takes a village." Likewise, we are indebted to our proofreader-moonlighting colleague and APA style fact checker, Kristal King, for her meticulous editing skills in the weeks leading up to submission. Indeed, we would likely still be scratching our heads without her tireless work ethic and relentless attention to detail.

Lastly, we would be remiss in not acknowledging our home institution, California State University, Long Beach, for the countless opportunities to reframe the challenges and frustrations we each faced over the years in our respective positions as topics of provocative praxis.

1 HIps in Hindsight, HIPS in Foresight

A Social-Justice Reimagining of Internships in the 21st Century

High-impact practice ("HIPs") pedagogy has graced pedagogical nomenclature since the mid-2000s, yet the interest in and scholarship on HIPs for college students only recently has soared, particularly where access to and participation in them by underserved student populations are concerned (Finley & McNair, 2013). In times of social upheaval and turbulence—#MeToo, Black Lives Matter, and Indigenous Land rights movement—ensuing crises are a rude awakening for our collective unconscious, inciting and invoking our humanity in spite of (and due to) their inherent nature. Indeed, in 1959, soon-to-be President John F. Kennedy uttered these words during the United Negro College Fund convocation: "When written in Chinese, the word 'crisis' is composed of two characters—one represents danger, and one represents opportunity" (Langan-Riekhof et al., 2017, para. 1). Although fact checkers would later discredit his flawed translation, the word nevertheless retains these dual implications, as Maria Langan-Riekhof et al. (2017), representing the Brookings Institution, assert:

> Out of crises can emerge new and incredible opportunities, particularly if traditional approaches and paradigms are questioned and challenged. During a crisis, incentives and motivations change, potentially leading to new cooperative behaviors and even to the creation of new systems or structures.
>
> (para. 2)

Crises as a phenomenon, then, are also capable of generating potential, inciting improvement, and sparking innovation. A crisis, more than a moment of intense difficulty, is an opportunity to make a choice.

The current conversations around HIPs are, in essence, a biproduct of crises. Ashley Finley and Tia McNair (2013) invoke a more benign phrase—"critical gaps"—citing a three-fold critical confluence facing internships:

> Scant evidence about the relationship between underserved students' learning and their engagement in high-impact practices . . . little is known

DOI: 10.4324/9781003296324-1

about whether engagement in these practices differentially affects learning outcomes for these and other traditionally underserved students ... what is known about the nature of student experiences with high-impact practices comes almost entirely from surveys, which often fail to reflect the rich detail that is present when students articulate, in their own voices, what these experiences mean to them in the context of their lives, their learning, and their hopes for obtaining a degree.

(p. 2)

InternsHIPs, too, is a rumination about crises that underscore the adage, "Necessity is the mother of invention." Our underserved students today are more vulnerable yet more eager to be empowered than ever. By questioning and aggressively exposing the systemic issues that beleaguer them, we can move toward educational policy reform at all levels. But first, where, when, and how did internships—those well-intended opportunities—go astray? Ross Perlin (2011) offers a potential answer:

Internships are a world of spin. And the reason you can spin them—whether you're an intern or an employer—is that no one knows what they mean. Internships may be everywhere today, but they remain such a recent, chaotic phenomenon that there are seldom any rules of the road, any standards or codes of conduct that are honored—only vague expectations, for which no one is accountable.

(p. xi)

As such, a combination of history and chronic, flagrant, human oversight may shed some light.

Any retrospect of HIPs should lead with George Kuh, the foremost expert on college internships and the Director of the National Institute for Learning Outcomes Assessment. Kuh, who coined the term around 2007 and whose pioneering research is unparalleled, has shaped the way we understand and implement these student-forward, experiential learning practices on college campuses. His seminal *High-Impact Educational Practices: What They Are, Who Has Access to Them, and Why They Matter* was the first to delineate the types of practices considered "high-impact," those ten or so opportunities that involve integrative learning—including internships, the focus of this book (Kuh, 2008).

Moving from theory toward practice, Kuh and O'Donnel (2013) outline in *Ensuring Quality & Taking High-Impact Practices to Scale* what individuals vital to the experience (e.g., students, faculty, supervisors, agencies, etc.) must adhere in order for a HIP to earn its title: high-level and appropriate performance expectations; significant investment of time and effort by students over an extended period of time; interactions with faculty and peers about substantive matters; experiences with diversity; frequent, timely, and constructive feedback; periodic and structured time to reflect on and integrate learning; discovery learning through real-world applications; and public demonstration of competence. HIPness could thus be qualified through the degree of simultaneity of Four I's—intensity, intention, interaction, and integration—whereby the omission of just one "I" can dilute the student experience.

As we explore the contours of HIPs, we recognize students' efforts and willingness are only as good as the circumstances—often highly specific, culturally determined, and financially bound—that enable (or stifle) intrinsic motivation as part of the HIP equation. Likewise, we acknowledge that the term "HIP" merely qualifies a concept, which is contingent upon and denotes the caliber of an experience that signals the degree of HIPness, and as John Zilvinskis (2019) points out, "studies only examine the role of participation in HIPs, not the overall quality of the experience" (p. 688). Or, as Hatch et al. (2016) aver, "the term *high-impact practices* proposes a hypothesis to be tested, a call to gather evidence to verify the claim of impact and to explore the experience of individuals and institutions in pursuing them" (p. 16). In other words, a "high impact" *label* does not guarantee a high-impact *experience*.

Kuh and O'Donnel (2013) lamentably but perhaps unsurprisingly are less likely to have access to or engage in HIPs, but when they do, they reap more benefits, a finding that in large part is the catalyst for our book (Kuh, 2008; Finley & McNair, 2013). Indeed, *InternsHIPs* uses Kuh's insightful (social-science) findings as a point of departure to further flesh out the equally important (humanistic) contours and nuances of HIPs from a pressing—if not compulsory—EDI perspective in the twenty-first century. While many of the internship and EDI topics included in our book have been studied, to greater and lesser degrees, they are typically addressed in isolation from each other. We uphold that in the context of HIPs like internships, these topics must all have a seat and voice at the table. Our book unapologetically positions these topics into critical conversation with each other, and, as a result, compels campus stakeholders to (re)consider the complexities of any internship program, from the fledgling to the already established, in the name of student success. In this way, our manuscript represents a compelling continuation of Kuh's ideas as we dialogue with them not only to reinforce his criteria for high-impact-related student success but also to suggest that the multi-layered concept is only possible when it transpires under certain qualifiable, quantifiable, and interconnected conditions. As we brainstormed the dimensions of these critical conversations, questions greatly outnumbered answers, which initially gave us reason for pause. But as each inquiry became more nuanced and layered, we realized that they were not part of the problem but rather at the heart of the "solution," both of which bear circumstantial-specific markings. More precisely, we wondered why we falter—particularly those in leadership positions—during such discussions or, worse yet, why we avoid them altogether. Discomfort, which invariably recalls Freud's pleasure principle, as well as a brief essay by Foucault (2000) in *Power*, "For an Ethic of Discomfort," became our prime suspect. A more practical, philosophical understanding of the term comes from feminist sociologist Rachelle Chadwick's (2021) recent essay, "On the Politics of Discomfort." Although Chadwick (2021) writes in the context of feminist epistemology, her ideas on gender justice are applicable to our own efforts, given that the labor of feminism to ensure gender equity has much in common with the equity issues our students confront, particularly Students of Color. We have since embraced the audacity of question-asking, as we see it as the obligatory first step in creating sustainable, authentic, student-forward internship programs and in the process have conceived a compelling neologism, "provocative praxis." This space of discomfort, which Chadwick (2021) recounts as "acknowledging, and staying with, messy ambivalences, sticky discomforts, falterings, disconnections, epistemic uncertainty and the intense feelings often evoked" is thus where provocative praxis, ironically, is most comfortable and productive (p. 559). As Hal Gregersen (2018) affirms, this could be because "Brainstorming for questions rather than answers makes it easier to push past cognitive biases and venture into unchartered territory" (p. 5). Although the *Oxford Online Dictionary* (2014) defines *provocative* as that which is "intended to make people angry or upset; intended to make people argue about something," our usage goes a step further by reframing any contention that arises as part of the productivity and resolution it incites. It is in this way that we approach some of the most pressing, systemic, twenty-first century issues (see "crises") facing internships today, as we acknowledge that not all programs and the experiences they entail are created equally or with equitable mindsets.

These are the ground rules for provocative praxis. Our book welcomes rather than shuns turbulent conversations. Indeed, *InternsHIPs* asks tough questions without providing easy answers (e.g., "*Are unpaid internships ethical?*"), as our previous use of "solutions" in quotations infers. Its pages include complex, problem-based, equity-minded scenarios instead of simple (or simplistic) remedies that minimize discomfort ("*Maricela, a Latina junior journalism major, works full-time and is struggling to accommodate her mandatory internship in her senior year*"). Its suggestions are applicable only when considering a particular campus' reality (e.g., budgetary opportunities and constraints, size, designation(s), and infrastructures). While these issues initially may muddle the conversation, they ultimately invite wonder, spark intrigue, and heighten curiosity as part of messy-by-default, inquiry-based learning. More importantly, they instigate action. This, we contend, is the true art of provocation, that which is at once is familiar (the sometimes grim but improvable realities) yet unfamiliar (the contextualized possibilities). Provocation at its core, then, is critical thinking with an edge.

Provocative praxis invites us to question, challenge, dismantle, and ultimately reform systems of injustice. The term was born at the crossroads of critical thinking, innovation, and a deep reverence for language during this project's infancy. By prioritizing its regenerative connotations (e.g., to agitate or inspire excitedly) as applied to systemic issues (internship related or otherwise), productivity displaces fear. Despite its alliterative whimsicality, make no mistake: provocative praxis in practice is complex, discomfiting, and exigent. It demands slow (albeit urgent) and deliberate thinking, nuanced conversations, holistic understandings, strategic advances, a willingness to learn (even in the throes of failure), and genuine collaborative commitments. What makes provocative praxis so unique and formidable is that it is contingent upon these demands, which will naturally vary from campus to campus, being met. Otherwise, all claims to "equity" languish, and we revert to "(bad) business as usual." In the end, provocative praxis is not about finger pointing or blame placing but instead advances the idea of knowing and doing better. As Jill Blackmore (2014) asserts, "being critical is more than just doing critique, as social change that leads to equity also requires informing policy and practice through advocacy and activism" (p. 499).

In the spirit of disruption, *InternsHIPs* strives to break all outdated, non-inclusive molds and their silo cousins. As such, it bears mentioning what this book is *not*: while students could (and should) read this book, *InternsHIPs* is intended for stakeholders, namely faculty, community agencies, and campus staff and administrators, whose classes, partnerships, and resources, respectively, ultimately coalesce to determine the integrity of internship processes and practices vis-à-vis provocative praxis. As such, it boasts a unique cross-division applicability. Furthermore, our book proposes (and argues for) a systemic approach that factors in the social, economic, and cultural challenges faced by college students today for a more holistic understanding of internships and the interns they purport to benefit. We thus encourage stakeholders to build programs that enlighten through the art of provocation, with all the broad applicability it entails. By posing provocative questions—ones that stimulate truthful, honest, transparent dialogue and require problem solving informed by institutional realities—intercampus stakeholders and partnering agencies are more compelled to engage in robust, comprehensive conversations about their respective programs.

Likewise, *InternsHIPs* is not a how-to, one-size-fits-all, cookie-cutter guide or manual. In that same vein, it does not include templates or classroom-inspired exercises or activities, which we see as prescriptive tools. While these do have a place in the context of internships (and elsewhere), we assert that provocation must always precede prescription because institutional realities and resources vary. Understanding and working within those parameters, or seeking to change them, is the key to effective and sustainable outcomes. For example, *Political Science Internships: Towards Best Practices* (American Political Science Association, 2021), while a sound resource for students, assumes an explicit, vocational perspective and adopts an overtly prescriptive approach to internships without alluding to provocative practice *first*. We liken this process to a physician recommending a medication without rendering a diagnosis. Similarly, books such as *Internships, Service Learning, and*

Volunteering Abroad: Successful Models and Best Practices (Nolting et al., 2013), *The Ultimate Guide to Internships: 100 Steps to Get a Great Internship and Thrive in It* (Woodard, 2015) and even the broader-promising *High-Impact Practices in Online Education: Research and Best Practices* (Linder & Mattison Hayes, 2018) are, by virtue of their titles, restrictively applicable, as "best practices" and "guides" are only as good as the provocative praxis that precedes them. Furthermore, we suspect that many of these so-called "practices," unfortunately, are imbued with and originate from places of (white) privilege. Our book, in contrast, tackles the big questions provocatively, holistically, and at their root, a necessary step if we are eventually to envision new models and solutions aimed at removing obstacles to equitable participation in internships for all students. In order to do this, we subscribe to Reeves' (2018) ideas in his riveting book, *Dream Hoarders*. His two salient points include acknowledging privilege when applicable: "The upper middle class has been having it pretty good. It is time those of us in the favored fifth recognize our privileged position. Some humility and generosity is required" (Reeves, 2018, p. 4); and engaging in hoisting from below: "The goal should be to level *up*: to help less advantaged parents invest more in their children and to make additional public investments in those children who have been unlucky in their parents" (Reeves, 2018, p. 46).

We expect the aforementioned conversation(s), therefore, to take us to raw, uncomfortable yet liberating, innovative places. In exchange for open-mindedness and trust, we exemplify how to transition from spaces of instability to places of thoughtful, holistic, and sustainable productivity. As the saying goes and as is often the case with amelioration measures, *things may worsen before they improve*. Exacerbation further embodies our usage of "provocative praxis," which we reference and implement throughout the book, in conjunction with recent EDIA (equity, diversity, inclusion, and access) scholarship, to prioritize the myriad challenges facing internships to arrive at equitable student success.

Understanding the history and evolution of internships, we believe, is the first step in addressing internship inequities. Olivia B. Waxman (2018), in her *Time* article "How Internships Replaced the Entry-Level Job," provides a succinct overview of internships, from their inception during the Middle Ages as "apprenticeships" to their present-day conceptualization as a structured, temporary, academically adjacent, supervised work experience. She likewise traces their association in the fields of medicine and law, both of which involved a palpable mentoring component (which may or may not be part of the contemporary internship experience, a topic we discuss later). Most importantly, as many economic historians have done before her, Waxman cites a 1947 Supreme Court Ruling, which provided a loophole to the The Fair Labor Standards Act (FSLA) a decade earlier, as the first watershed moment that "helped future employers justify unpaid internships" (para. 6). A second turning point occurred in the 1970s, as college enrollments (and demand for internships) skyrocketed, and job market competition stiffened. As Waxman states, internships were thought to give graduates an edge. The workforce landscape shifted yet again in the early 2000s, as interns, perhaps incited by empowering social-justice movements, intrepidly began to denounce workplace exploitation, particularly in the case of unpaid internships. Although the Department of Labor, in response to one high-profile lawsuit, updated the 81-year-old Fair Labor Standards Act in 2018, the changes merely agitated the internship waters by relaxing the Act's terms. The result is a system that makes it even easier for businesses to "use"—a verb we use intentionally—unpaid interns (Waxman, 2018).

This negligent oversight within internship programs, what Ross Perlin (2011) calls a "blind spot" (p. 63), thus begs a related question: are campuses internship-ready? We suspect that most, regrettably, are not, despite operating as such. Kuh et al. (2011) provide a checklist of sorts, as well as cites (and mandates) "four key conditions for sustaining good work in hard times," understood here as institutions that embody internship readiness: (1) An ethic of positive restlessness permeates the campus. (2) Data about students and their success inform deliberations and decisions about the curriculum and other institutional priorities. (3) Academic and student affairs staff collaborate to foster student success cases. (4) Campus leaders work assiduously to increase the numbers of faculty and staff who understand the importance of and become committed to student success (pp. 2–3). Our applause for Kuh's insight is directly proportional to his suggestive word choice: "hard times" (p. 1), "work assiduously" (p. 3), and "positive restlessness" (p. 3). Without expressly saying so, Kuh hints that running internship programs is a consistently collaborative and labor-intensive endeavor (and that by association, campuses might not be functioning in this way, either deliberately or unintentionally). The key is to recognize when we aren't and to react (p. 8).

In *Student Success in College: Creating Conditions That Matter*, Kuh et al. (2010) add the student element to the mix:

> Student engagement has two key components that contribute to student success. The first is the amount of time and effort students put into their studies and activities that lead to the experiences and outcomes that constitute student success. The second is the way the institution allocates resources and organizes learning opportunities and services to induce students to participate in and benefit from such activities.
>
> (p. 9)

This information alone elucidates why internships are not and should not be conceived as merely "on-the-job training" and that when they are, their status

8 HIPs in Hindsight, HIPs in Foresight

as a HIP is jeopardized by what Perlin (2011) calls "an avalanche of calculated voluntarism" (p. 107). Perlin at once illuminates and problematizes this issue:

> The term "intern" should be applied ethically and transparently to opportunities that involve training, mentoring, and getting to know a line of work—internships should reflect what a given industry is all about and what the organization actually does. Tasks should play to an intern's strengths and account for the training she's receiving.
>
> (p. 209)

Advocacy for paid internships is further bolstered by the National Association of College and Employers (NACE, n.d.), which states "Using an equity lens, NACE's position statement on unpaid internships is a call to policymakers to address the inherent inequities unpaid internships cause and to work to ensure all internships are paid" (para. 1), which underscores "the denunciatory yet reformation-seeking underpinnings of Perlin's exposé" (2011).

While student success is rightfully located at the intersection of intrinsic motivation and institutional infrastructure, we would be remiss to discount the inevitable speedbumps and potholes on this road to student success, as we have observed them firsthand. The traditional sacrifices we have asked students to make smack of inequity and often render themselves impossible. In that spirit, this student-minded book explores the spaces we've traditionally overlooked, either consciously or unconsciously, to look at student success from the student viewpoint, namely what constitutes it more holistically and leads to it fairly. For example, a highly motivated student has just secured a credit-bearing internship with a local non-profit. But if that student is a single mother working a tuition-dependent part-time job, do her financial losses outweigh the internship gains? This question becomes even more complex when students are required to complete an internship as part of their major requirements. We see our aim in this book to look at these situations with a growth mindset centered on reframing and re-envisioning to ensure that students not only engage in HIPs but that they do so in a way that is financially, personally, and emotionally viable to ultimately create academic internship programs that are at once responsible, sustainable, and advantageous. While a plethora of research exists on the data of HIPs, our book aims to better contextualize it, problematize it, and flesh it out in ways that give a face to the numbers in compelling, and, as our title suggests, provocative ways. As Kuh et al. (2010) assert, "This emphasizes the importance of being equity minded when scaling HIP participation. Which students are experiencing HIPs, and who is left out? Are underrepresented students having high-quality experiences? Access to HIPs without equitable participation is a hollow achievement" (para. 25).

Situating critical terms in the context of *Internships*

InternsHIPs refers to and relies on the interplay of several key, critical terms. Because these terms are often understood broadly or, in other cases, figure as neologisms, explicit definitions are warranted. As per our title, EDIA, "equity, diversity, inclusion, and access," is the fulcrum of the book; it is the concept that drives our thesis and that which, frankly, compelled us—three women working in the largest, most diverse state university system in the United States—to collaborate in the first place. At the extremes of the metaphorical pivot point are "provocative praxis" and "intersectionality." Because we see "equity" as an umbrella term subsuming the subcategories of "diversity" and "inclusion," we prioritize "equity" by default. After all, if a system is equitable, diversity and inclusion become inherent. In other words, while you can have a diverse and inclusive system that does not necessarily signal an equitable one (resulting in disingenuous outcomes). This idea of *leading* with equity, we should point out, has gained traction in and beyond academia, and, as such, we will use the acronym, EDIA.

Given that this book is steeped in equity, and because we have seen the term used haphazardly elsewhere—both performatively and too broadly—we want to be explicit about our own working definition. In the spirit of recognizing that equity is sometimes too inclusive for its own good and to its detriment, we thus subscribe to Estela Mara Bensimon's (2018) definition:

> Equity has a very strong and distinct meaning. It is rooted in achieving racial proportionality in all educational outcomes and in critically assessing whiteness at the institutional and practice levels. It is about acknowledging and addressing racism in our educational systems.
>
> (p. 98)

Like Bensimon (2018), who rightfully declares, "I want to reclaim the racial justice focus that is the rightful meaning and intent of equity," we, too, endeavor to recuperate the racial contours and dissect the systemic pillars of equity, particularly as they relate to and impact students (p. 95). Furthermore, we agree with Steven J. Ball (2017), who observes:

> Education policy in relation to "race" and racism is to a great extent only brought to the forefront at moments of "race crisis," and even then, typically is displaced into inquiries and reports and "enacted" through exhortation and good intentions rather than practical actions, and often subsumed within other standards-raising moves.
>
> (p. 188)

Bensimon (2018) offers complementary, actionable perspectives on equity, including "confronting the whitewashing of equity," reclaiming its "racial justice focus" and the underscoring of what we see as its two salient points

> Most of these national level reforms simply do not acknowledge racialization, racism, or whiteness, even as they avow a commitment to equity. These reforms insist on benefiting "all" students, even as the term "all" is not in line with equity work, nor does it typically lead white practitioners or policymakers to imagine specifically Black and Brown youths and adults.
>
> (p. 97)

and "Equity and equity-mindedness accept that it is whiteness—not the achievement gap—that produces and sustains racial inequality in higher education" (p. 97). Indeed, whiteness fans the flames of inequity. While our book alone cannot atone for systemic abuse, the ideas therein may help People of Color and whites engage more productively for the greater good: our Students of Color.

Intersectionality, we contend, at once elevates and escalates the equity conversation. In light of and in response to FLSA's loosened criteria, combined with the general lack of quality control over internships nationwide, we are particularly anxious to probe the manifold, intersectional manifestations of equity, hereafter referred to as "intersequity," whereby an individual's intersectionality (in this case, that of students) interfaces with and can exacerbate inequitable practices. In her article on equity-minded high-impact learning, Valerie Chepp (2017) at once explains and exemplifies that "Especially at risk are students from historically marginalized or underserved groups, including underrepresented minority, first-generation, transfer, and/or low-income students" (p. 163). These equity groups assume secondary dimensions when we factor in additional identifying markers including but not limited to sexuality, gender, ethnicity, abilities, and faith. We invite our readers, for instance, to consider the myriad barriers facing students who identify in the following ways: a young, gay, first-generation Black man; a Latina student-mother who works part-time; an Asian-American Muslim transfer student; a Two-Spirit, differently abled Native American student. While equity, as Bensimon (2018) states, should be grounded in Brown and Blackness, examining it through an intersectional lens only brings those bodies into focus.

Our integration of social-justice-oriented research, therefore, includes an intentionally tapered, historically driven definition of "equity" as well as a simultaneous incorporation of broader categories of access, participation, and rights to help ensure that HIP endeavors strive for abundance and proceed with generosity. We illustrate this idea through some of the most recent, forward-thinking scholarship by some of the most prominent scholars in their respective fields.

The Experiential Learning Cycle (Kolb, 1984), involves four, evolving, knowledge-yielding phases called the "transformation of experience," whereby "Learning is the process whereby knowledge is created through the transformation of experience" (p. 38). Tara J. Yosso's (2005) community cultural wealth model similarly helps reframe and reimagine student social capital by subverting deficit thinking (i.e., focusing on attributes rather than lack). Yosso's ideas, in turn, complement Museus' (2014) culturally engaging campus environment model to ultimately question if (perhaps unexpectedly) the omission of explicit reference to equity and inclusion in defining key elements of HIPs unintentionally has contributed to the issues facing internship-eligible students. Each chapter will enjoy a robust interspersing of social-justice scholarship relevant to its respective focus.

Interns are the *sin qua non* to internships. Therefore, when even one part of their support system is overlooked, minimized, or omitted, and/or if the benefit burden is misdirected, the integrity of the internship is compromised. Given that human beings are at the heart of internships, two biology terms—mutualism and parasitism—seem fitting to describe and understand internships in tertiary education. *Parasitism*, as the name suggests, confers a benefit to one organism (the parasite) while concurrently doing harm to the other (the host).

A contradiction of terms, parasitic internships nevertheless exist and persist. Perlin's (2011) tongue-in-cheek chapter, "The happiest interns in the world" in *Intern Nation* offers blistering evidence, enough to qualify the Disney internship experience as "a term of indenture" (p. 3). On a less flagrant level, anecdotes about students who chronically engage in mindless, menial chores (as opposed to meaningful, developmental, and associative work) while interning abound: the coffee maker, the lunch retriever; the intern whose only bragging right at summer's end was having mailed four thousand flyers. Perlin (2011) calls this "intern abuse," which includes everything from "wiping down door handles" to "dressing in gorilla suits for a birthday" (pp. 68–69). To ask an intern (or an employee) to tend to one of these periodically may be acceptable, particularly if there is an office or culture that involves all staff, but these should not be an intern's regular responsibilities because they are not feedback worthy nor do they have a link to a student's academic program, major, or career aspirations. Likewise, parasitic internships, as the adjective implies, syphon from the student in a way that primarily, if not solely, benefits the agency. Perlin's exposé exemplifies what happens when certain internships persist and go unchecked: "The internship program at Disney World is what keeps it running" (p. xvi). Perlin (2011) adds that thousands of college students work full-time and for minimum wage there every year and that they "work entirely at the company's will, subject to a raft of draconian politics, without sick days or time off, without grievance procedures, without guarantees of workers' compensation or protection against harassment or unfair treatment" (p. 2). In other words, on paper these are interns, but in practice, they are exploited employees. As a result, the practice ceases to be an internship by default. As we underscore throughout this book, a teamwork approach helps regulate such abuse as it affects Students of Color, for whom parasitic internships are particularly deleterious.

Mutualism, in contrast, underscores advantageousness, harmony, and fairness. Mutualism, then, is the benchmark for all HIPs and how we argue internships should be conceived and considered: as a symbiotic, interwoven, connected parts-to-a-whole, teaching and learning experience. The equality or sameness the word infers drives the intersecting relationships that maximize the quality of experience as well as student benefit burden. Much like drones and worker bees who ensure the stability of a shared hive by instinctively serving the queen, a team of humans works to safeguard and support the intern. It is this spirit of collaboration that embodies, informs, and drives *InternsHIPs*.

Leadership frames: a call to arms

Bolman and Gallos' (2011) concept of four frames of leadership buttresses students' transformative experiences in this EDIA context because, as we see it, *IntersHIPs* is fundamentally a summons to (intrepid) leadership. Equity is at worst unattainable and at best performative without infrastructure and innovation, both of which start in higher (Ed) echelons. An understanding and assurance of each of these frames independently as well as collectively are paramount to any organization's health and growth.

The structural frame describes approaches that rely heavily on, as its name infers, the structure of work, the organizations of which they are part, and the change process (Bolman & Gallos, 2011, p. 53). The structural frame likewise champions time management and prioritization of workflow; creates systems and procedures; delineates strategy; sets goals; determines responsibilities and reporting lines; and proposes common metrics. The political frame builds coalitions, engages negotiation, and sets agendas in an effort to recognize stakeholders, their interests, and their positionality (Bolman & Gallos, 2011, pp. 77–80). As such, it also leverages allies. The human resources frame values open communication, empowerment, allyship, coaching and care, and hiring the right people (Bolman & Gallos, 2011, p. 94). This frame encourages conciliation, values teamwork, and embraces humanistic endeavors. The symbolic frame, although most elusively conceived and defined, as one would expect from symbols, has an important function in an organization as the accoutrement of visionaries, example setters, heroic narrators, and leverage seekers who inspire and galvanize (Bolman & Gallos, 2011, p. 117).

Most individuals think of these frames as independent approaches (if they think of them at all), while effective leaders know which frames they identify with most readily and which lie outside their wheelhouse. Being aware of our own strengths and weaknesses as leaders, although perhaps contradictory, is key to working intentionally to engage the frames a situation solicits for maximum output and outcomes. This book, through internship-adjacent scenarios, elucidates how each frame functions, both independently and collectively, to conciliatorily explore and address the unwieldy issues related to provocative praxis. Bolman and Gallos (2011) assert that instilling hope, understood as "strong faith, solid thinking, creativity, willful action and persistence in the face of the unknown," is a leader's underlying duty (p. 218).

Like us, Bolman and Gallos (2011) are serendipitously interested in perspectivism and lenses: "Strong academic leaders are skilled in the art of *reframing*—a deliberate process of shifting perspectives to see the same situation in multiple ways and through different lenses" (p. 13). Reframing is interested in "alternative views," "sensemaking," and suspending the human propensity to fall into indolent pattern-thinking. Bolman and Gallos call this "breaking frame," disrupting even the most general script in way allows us to move toward more effective resolutions (Bolman & Gallos, 2011, pp. 23–28). The authors provide an extreme but useful example of a frame break: imagine a gun-wielding intruder disrupts your intimate dinner party with friends (Bolman & Gallos, 2011, pp. 28–29). A frame break would manifest as inviting the trespasser to a glass of wine rather than displaying a defensive reaction. Imagine this, now, in a HIPs context using the previous single-mother example. Instead of encouraging her to change majors, which could prove personally catastrophic by having her incur an additional loan burden or postpone graduation, a reframing-oriented leader might help her secure a paid internship or determine if her current job could be repurposed into one. Whether you call it thinking outside the box, lateral thinking or pushing the envelope, this unconventional process is often the fairest way forward when considering the complex, if not complicated, lives of the twenty-first century college students. After all, as the authors state, "Leadership works when relationships work" (Bolman & Gallos, 2011, p. 46). Using Bolman and Gallos' (2011) concept of four frames, overall, informs scaling and sustaining institution-wide internship initiatives, which all must do, but which only healthy ones can.

The internship topics that comprise this book (e.g., partnerships, infrastructure, assessment, etc.) adhere to a uniform, three-fold structure per chapter with dynamic, complementary parts. We anchor each to a real-world (nonfictional) case study, which interweaves throughout the chapter and facilitates discussion of the themes and key issues from an equity perspective. The case studies highlight the process to turn a problem into a prototype, with all the provocative praxis and adaptability one entails. We then punctuate the case studies with ancillary (fictional) scenarios, such as the ones referenced earlier in this chapter. The questions the case study yields give way to what we call "Big Picture Issues" (BPIs), which we exemplify through "provocation in practice." These figure as connections, patterns, and behaviors inherent to internship practices. The third and culminating piece, "Theory to Practice"

(TTP), offers a wide array of conciliatory questions and answers—not to be confused with prescriptive "solutions"—within the overarching EDIA framework of the book.

For the sake of transparency and due to the critical nature of provocative praxis (and the exposure involved), some interviewees declined to go on record with their own institutional hurdles. We wonder why some lead with a defense—we suspect retaliatory acts—rather than engage in forthcoming, albeit difficult, conversations. In these cases, we have honored anonymity and write in more general terms as middle ground to balance requests for privacy with our need for content. In contrast, some leaders, including Tracey Lord (Florida State University) and Kathleen Powell (College of William and Mary), were eager to discuss the challenges on their respective campuses. They appreciated that we "spoke their language," which made them feel validated and seen. This divide signals a provocative praxis moment: if we are all, essentially, working toward the same goals, shouldn't we interpret the challenges on our respective campuses as a means to an end? After all, only in this way can we reflect on what these critical conversations must, by definition, entail. In the meantime, we embrace the hesitancy, as it is a glaring reminder that *InternsHIPs* is doing its part in advancing the scholarship that promotes equitable internships. Leaning into best practices—and obsoleting their less-than-optimal counterparts, we argue—is only possible if we are willing first to engage in provocative praxis.

Chapter 2, "Institutional infrastructure: centralization, workload, collaboration, and funding," tackles long-standing and, contrastively, neglected questions surrounding infrastructural support for programming that ensures equitable student access to and participation in internships. It opens with a discussion of the strong senior leadership needed for sustaining and scaling internship efforts. The chapter also addresses the debate of whether to centralize internship practices, the struggles associated with collaborating within and between divisions, the feminization and isolation of internship work, funding streams necessary to support paid internship placements, and our campus policies and procedures governing internships that continue to disadvantage students.

Chapter 3, "Intersequity, Students of Color, and the perils of unpaid internships," explores the neologism "intersequity," where intersectionality meets equity, as a compulsory element of the student internship experience. It questions if scholars in the white tower of privilege have overlooked important factors when determining what constitutes a HIP. Likewise, it reinforces the idea of checks and balances in internship program government. The chapter culminates with a proposal to outlaw unpaid internships, which do nothing more than benefit students who can already afford to undertake one and disadvantage (at best) or exclude (at worst) those who do not have the luxury of working for free.

Chapter 4, "Community partners as critical coefficients in the internship equation," asserts who has a seat at the table matters and often internship partners are excluded from this process. We examine how lack of open communication and transparency impedes the universities' ability to cultivate authentic partnerships with internship sites. We explore examples of how to train site supervisors who provide critical mentoring and support to interns, and the role that community partners can play in shaping university internship curriculum. Unique to this chapter, we could not find a single case study that could be woven throughout. Instead, we showcase various examples that highlight each section, and underscore the point that there is no one-size-fits-all approach to cultivating partnerships.

Chapter 5, "Assessment as a catalyst for addressing equity in internships," addresses the importance of internship assessment, including the centering of student voices using mixed method approaches and forging collaborations across divisions and units to share data. We highlight national surveys and more local assessment efforts like surveys, focus groups, and the use of students' photos and narratives as we discuss the need to move beyond tracking which students complete internships and who is hosting our students to better understand how students experience these (supposed) HIPs. We also address analytic challenges to using assessment data to inform targeted program improvements.

The Afterword, on an auspicious note, envisions the next steps and proposes ways—through collaborative and strategic endeavors, persistence, and honesty—to bring them to fruition.

In this interconnected, student-equity-forward way, *InternsHIPs* rightfully and urgently demands bold, public disruptions of the way we envisage, structure, and resource college internships while it simultaneously impresses upon us the pervasiveness of long-standing barriers. If Perlin (2011) throws down the gauntlet—"educators are in a position to initiate positive, momentous changes"—we (must) rise to the occasion (p. 215). For the sake of student success, confronting and reconciling correlated issues of equity must be our first, if not most important, action item if college internship programs stand a chance.

References

American Political Science Association. (2021, September 1). *Political science internships: Towards best practices* (R. B. Van Vechten, B. Gentry, & C. J. Berg, Eds.). American Political Science Association.

Ball, S. J. (2017). *The education debate* (3rd ed.). Policy Press. https://doi.org/10.2307/j.ctt1t893tk

Bensimon, E. M. (2018). Reclaiming racial justice in equity. *Change: The Magazine of Higher Learning, 50*(3–4), 95–98. https://doi.org/10.1080/00091383.2018.1509623

Blackmore, J. (2014). Cultural and gender politics in Australian education, the rise of edu-capitalism and the 'fragile project' of critical educational research. *The Australian Educational Researcher*, *41*(5), 499–520. https://doi.org/10.1007/s13384-014-0158-8

Bolman, L. G., & Gallos, J. V. (2011). *Reframing academic leadership*. Jossey-Bass.

Chadwick, R. (2021). On the politics of discomfort. *Feminist Theory*, *22*(4), 556–574. https://doi.org/10.1177/1464700120987379

Chepp, V. (2017). Equity-minded high-impact learning: A short-term approach to student-faculty collaborative research. *Humboldt Journal of Social Relations*, *39*, 163–175. https://doi.org/10.55671/0160-4341.1017

Finley, A., & McNair, T. (2013). *Assessing underserved students' engagement in high-impact practices*. Association of American Colleges and Universities.

Foucault, M. (2000). For an ethics of discomfort. In J. D. Faubion (Ed.), *Power: Essential works of Foucault, 1954–1984* (Vol. III, pp. 443–448). The New Press.

Gregersen, H. (2018). Better brainstorming. *Harvard Business Review*, *96*(2), 64–71.

Hatch, D. K., Crisp, G., & Wesley, K. (2016, September 2). What's in a name? The challenge and utility of defining promising high-impact practices. *New Directions for Community Colleges*, *2016*(175), 9–17. https://doi.org/10.1002/cc.20208

Kolb, D. A. (1984). *Experiential learning: Experience as the source of learning and development*. Prentice-Hall.

Kuh, G. D. (2008). High-impact educational practices: What they are, who has access to them, and why they matter. *Peer Review*, *14*(3), 29.

Kuh, G. D., Kinzie, J., Schuh, J. H., & Whitt, E. J. (2010). *Student success in college: Creating conditions that matter*. Jossey-Bass. (Original work published 2005)

Kuh, G. D., Kinzie, J., Schuh, J. H., & Whitt, E. J. (2011, July/August). Fostering student success in hard times. *Change*, *43*(4), 13–19. https://doi.org/10.1080/00091383.2011.585311

Kuh, G. D., & O'Donnell, K. (2013). *Ensuring quality & taking high-impact practices to scale*. Association of American Colleges & Universities [AAC&U]. aacu.org

Langan-Riekhof, M., Avanni, A. B., & Janetti, A. (2017, April 10). *Sometimes the world needs a crisis: Turning challenges into opportunities*. Brookings Institute.

Linder, K. E., & Mattison Hayes, C. (Eds.). (2018). *High-impact practices in online education: Research and best practices*. Routledge. https://doi.org/10.4324/9781003445104

Museus, S. D. (2014). The Culturally Engaging Campus Environments (CECE) Model: A new theory of college success among racially diverse student populations. In M. B. Paulsen (Ed.), *Higher education: Handbook of theory and research* (pp. 189–227). Springer. https://doi.org/10.1007/978-94-017-8005-6_5

National Association of Colleges and Employers. (n.d.). *Unpaid internships and the need for federal action. Position Statement: U.S. Internships*. naceweb.org

Nolting, W., Donohue, D., Matherly, C., & Tillman, M. J. (Eds.). (2013). *Internships, service learning, and volunteering abroad: Successful models and best practices*. NAFSA: Association of International Educators.

Oxford Online Dictionary. (2014). *Provocative*. Retrieved 2022, from www.oxforddictionaries.com/

Perlin, R. (2011). *Intern nation: How to earn nothing and learn little in the brave new economy*. Verso.

Reeves, R (2017). *Dream Hoarders: How the American Upper Middle Class is Leaving Everyone Else in the Dust, Why that is a Problem, and What to Do About It.* Brookings Institute Press.

Waxman, O. B. (2018, July 25). How internships replaced the entry-level job. *Time.* https://time.com/5342599/history-of-interns-internships/

Woodard, E. (2015). *The ultimate guide to internships: 100 steps to get a great internship and thrive in it.* Allworth Press.

Yosso, T. J. (2005). Whose culture has capital? A critical race theory discussion of community cultural wealth. *Race Ethnicity and Education, 8*(1), 69–91. https://doi.org/10.1080/1361332052000341006

Zilvinskis, J. (2019). Measuring quality in high-impact practices. *Higher Education, 78*(4), 87–709. https://doi.org/10.1007/s10734-019-00365-9

2 Institutional Infrastructure

Centralization, Workload, Collaboration & Funding

I hope it goes without saying that institution wide internship programs require more than mission statements: they're a real monetary investment. If a college or university wants to engage all students in internships then they also have to wonder what it would look like for internship offices to be well resourced and operated by an administrator with an institution wide mandate to lead, outside of any particular school or program. To be frank, it probably looks expensive.

(Langemak, 2022, para. 11)

Indeed, sound institutional infrastructure lays the necessary groundwork for equitable student access to and participation in internships. This chapter addresses several components of institutional infrastructure including strong senior leadership, centralization, faculty and staff workload, collaborations across divisions, funding streams, and policies and procedures governing internships. Unfortunately, publications and discourse specific to building institutional infrastructure to sustain and scale internship programming are scant. We incorporate the research where it does exist, but often must extrapolate from substantive areas outside of internship programming like human resource management, and share examples from our own internship work at the California State University, Long Beach, and other universities like Idaho State University. Because we are exploring uncharted territories, there are a plenty of opportunities for provocative praxis—we ask questions and encourage innovative thinking as it relates to these issues. We also highlight the multitude of ways that infrastructural issues dovetail with Bolman and Gallos' (2011) four leadership frames: symbolic, human resources, structural, and political.

Strong senior leadership

Having placed over 9,000 students in paid internships as part of their Career Path Internship Program (CPIP), Emily Jahsman, Associate Director of the Career Center at Idaho State University (n.d.), knows that sustaining and scaling institution-wide internship programs begin with strong senior leadership. Creating infrastructural support and a culture that fosters collaboration is a senior leadership responsibility. The effort cannot be "bottom up," led by faculty and staff who do not have the access or decision-making power to commit resources to the effort.

But what does strong senior leadership look like in the internship landscape? At the most basic level, we need administrators who are willing and able to engage in the self-reflective work necessary for identifying personal and institutional biases, campus messaging, and institutional infrastructures (or lack thereof) that may support systemic inequities in internship participation. For example, leaders need to reconcile aggressive campus messaging and advising policies that prioritize four-year graduation (a laudable goal that we know decreases students' loan burden) with articulated strategic priorities that encourage students to complete professional internships before graduating. Many students who must work to support themselves and pay tuition (often low-income Students of Color) cannot do both—graduate in four years and complete even short-term professional internships. Far too often these students are counseled out of completing internships, not because it is what is best for them, but because we are concerned about our four-year graduation rates and state funding tied to these rates.

We also need senior leaders willing to be transparent about their priorities and to publicly hold themselves accountable, even when it creates personal risk. Named the top public university for internships by the Princeton Review's *Best Value Colleges* (2023), William and Mary have sent a clear message (à la symbolic framing) that internships are a priority by pledging in their Vision 2026 strategic plan to provide a funded internship opportunity or other applied learning experience for every undergraduate. Similarly, our university (the California State University, Long Beach) has articulated its commitment to equitable internships by including explicit mention of them in our Beach 2030 strategic plan (CSULB University Strategic Communications, 2021) and providing seed money to initiate a university-level Academic Internships Office. Our Provost has also dedicated her Chief Operating Officer's time to assist with campus messaging, cross-division collaborations, and donor relations, a strong signal to our campus partners that our Provost is committed to resourcing, scaling, and sustaining internship programming on our campus. In perhaps the most public declaration of internship priorities, former Idaho State University President, Arthur Vailas, piloted in 2011 what was to become the Career Path Internship Program (Idaho State University, n.d.) by investing $250,000 from his general budget to pay internship wages for students completing internships. This initial investment has grown over the years and now tops $2 million annually.

While these examples are extraordinary, they nevertheless underscore what is possible when mouth meets money. If your campus is not yet ready to make equitable access to and participation in internships a priority, your leaders must own that. There is no shame in having other priorities that take precedence, but it is not acceptable to champion internships in strategic planning while simultaneously minimizing the need for institutional support for these efforts. In our research for this book, we talked with several internship program staff and faculty who told us that they continue to battle administrators' perceptions that their work is tangential to student success and by extension, not worthy of campus-wide resource investments. Staff are peppered with questions like, "Isn't everything we do at the university a high-impact practice?" and "Why do we need to call special attention to internships or resource them at the university level?" These questions demonstrate that there is still much to do in the way of educating campus leaders on the internship landscape. The dearth of studies published on administrators' perspectives on internships—unlike other HIPs—suggests that perhaps it is time to bring leaders into the fold along with the faculty and staff already there.

Administrative blind spots hamper any internship effort. For example, we have also heard repeatedly from senior management that sometimes you have to "build the plane while you fly it" and that after initial internship efforts have demonstrated their value, the university can be obligated to create institutional infrastructures and provide monetary support. We contend that this is a dangerous proposition, as successfully flying a half-built plane while you flesh out policies and procedures with limited (or no) staff can inadvertently send the message that resources are not needed. The plane seems fine so why invest in infrastructure? In these circumstances what is ignored is the heavy lifting done by individuals who, at great personal sacrifice and/ or expense, keep the plane flying, with hopes that demonstrating proof of concept will bring recognition and resources. Far too often those resources never come, and individuals who devoted their time and passion to initiating and sustaining internship efforts are left with a dilemma: Do they continue to prop up programs despite a lack of institutional support or do they allow these programs—along with their self-fueling passions—to wither and die?

Affirming the power of the pivot, senior leaders need to symbolically frame their commitment to equitable internship programming and set an example through their own behavior. Administrators' promotion of internships is only as good as their ability to fully understand and articulate what a true high-impact practice is, as well as the accompanying vision of those individuals who oversee campus-connected internships. Senior leaders must also be able to provide feedback about internship programming ideas without being dismissive, be open to (even encourage) feedback about their own plans and actions, and change their minds when evidence suggests a new direction is needed (Pisano, 2019). Creating safe spaces for provocative praxis is challenging in higher education (ironically) as faculty and staff are not typically trained to have difficult conversations and where disagreement is often viewed as unproductive, if not combative: "To challenge too strongly is to risk looking like you are not a team player" (Pisano, 2019, p. 68). This could represent an opportunity for administrators to engage in Conflict Transformation trainings (Botes, 2001) to understand that this tension, an offshoot of provocative praxis, is, in fact, beneficial. Acknowledging that at the heart of such discussions are issues and not people is key in advancing the marker.

In addition to downplaying the need for resources and infrastructure, we see a tendency among administrators to pathologize those willing to question what the university is doing, who insist we walk our talk (McNair et al., 2020), or who are impatient with the glacial pace of change on our campuses as it relates to ensuring equitable access to internships. Many of us (mostly women) have been told to "calm down" by senior administrators when we insist that our campuses can do more to address inequities in internship programming. Instead of resorting to sexist language and labeling those who make us uncomfortable as controversial and difficult, what would happen if instead we supported faculty and staff who are willing to navigate uncharted territory and hold us accountable?

Might we go so far as to identify and reward what LePeau (2015) calls social gadflies?

> The history of *gadfly* starts with *gad* which now means "chisel" but which formerly could designate a spike, spear, or rod for goading cattle. Late in the 16th century, *gad* was joined with *fly* to designate any of several insects that aggravate livestock. Before too long, we began applying *gadfly* to people who annoy or provoke others.
> (Merriam-Webster, n.d.)

While the term gadfly is typically used pejoratively, we could reclaim the term and use it to refer to those who do the admirable work of challenging those in positions of power who lead with a defense rather than an offense, questioning the status quo, and generating innovative solutions that address inequities in internship participation: "Unvarnished candor is critical to innovation because it is the means by which ideas evolve and improve" (Pisano, 2019, p. 68). Social gadflies could be given a seat at the table, a real voice in internship discussions, and the latitude to act.

In the spirit of being a reclaimed gadfly, we make a plea for administrators who create legitimized space and time to develop projects that challenge the typical way of "doing internships." As institutions of learning, it is ironic that we often navigate away from the process of learning when crafting initiatives. That is, we have little tolerance for failure, yet it is often trial and error that gives us insight into what works best for our students. We encourage the use of design thinking, "a non-linear, iterative process that teams use to understand users, challenge assumptions, redefine problems, and create innovative solutions to prototype, and test" (Interaction Design Foundation, n.d., para. 1). Tackling internship challenges using design thinking allows for prototyping and testing before we make substantial resource investments and institutional commitments to internship initiatives.

Pisano (2019) argues that tolerance for failure is not tolerance for incompetence. Prototyping innovative internship ideas that ultimately fail is acceptable and even expected, "but mediocre technical skills, sloppy thinking, bad work habits, and poor management are not" (p. 65). The key to successful design thinking as it relates to internship programming is for "senior leadership to articulate clearly the difference between productive and unproductive failures: Productive failures yield valuable information relative to their cost" (Pisano, 2019, p. 66).

Centralization

Once leaders have committed to providing infrastructural support for internship programming, one of the first issues to address—a structural leadership task— is whether to centralize efforts. While many resist centralization, there are aspects of the delivery of internships that, if coordinated across the institution, would leave more time for faculty and staff to focus on advancing equitable learning outcomes for students. But rather than advocate strictly for centralization, we wonder: Is there a way to adopt a blended model where we centralize some aspects of internships while honoring the diversity of approaches that have evolved over time due to specific college needs and accreditation requirements?

Perhaps one way to address partial centralization is to coordinate centrally those internship tasks that are value generating. That is, might we centralize aspects of internship programming that are not disciplinary specific, hold the potential to save money if centralized, and typically require expertise beyond the skill sets of most department, college, and program staff/ faculty? The assessment of internship outcomes is one area that lends itself to centralization and is the topic of Chapter 5.

Another area ripe for centralization is risk and liability management. With the growing concern about student safety and the legality of internships, many universities now require host sites (especially those not paying interns) to complete memos of understanding (MOUs) or Student Placement Agreements that outline hosting sites' responsibilities (e.g., qualified employees to supervise student interns) and rights (e.g., right to refuse participation to students who are not in good academic standing). These MOUs and agreements also typically identify the university's responsibilities and rights, required insurance by host sites (general liability and workers compensation coverage), confidentiality of student information, non-discrimination policies, and adherence to the Fair Labor Standards Act.

Campus Contract Services or Risk Management Offices typically handle the processing of MOUs, set the policy on their necessity, and retain the authority to sign agreements. Yet, without centralization, there is no formal connection between Contract Services/Risk Management and the faculty and staff who run internship programs and are responsible for managing campus partnerships with community organizations and businesses that host our interns. Instead, colleges and departments are typically left to figure out on their own how to initiate the MOUs (if they can even find them). We have heard from many faculty and staff that they do not understand the need for MOUs, the process of executing them, or why they do not have the authority to sign them. As a result of the confusion, many faculty and staff ignore the required paperwork and simply hope that nothing bad—from a slip and fall injury to a sexual harassment claim—happens. Or staff and faculty push the responsibility for executing these agreements onto students who have even less knowledge about why and how to handle MOUs. The result in both cases is that we have students completing internships with organizations and businesses that do not understand what we expect of them, who do not have the proper insurance to cover students in the event of an accident, and who are not legally bound to adhere to our campus policies on non-discrimination and inclusion.

Centralizing risk and liability would allow campuses to ensure that all students completing internships are protected. It also has the potential to reduce overall workload, redundancy, and burden on our collaborating community partners. When departments and colleges are required to initiate their own MOUs and Student Placement Agreements, community organizations that host students from multiple departments and colleges can find themselves in situations where they are asked to sign multiple agreements—we know of one hosting organization that had a dozen signed agreements with a single campus. This duplication is unnecessary and likely sends the message to our community partners that we are disorganized. Centralized risk management for internships would also allow campuses to respond more quickly to campus, regional, and worldwide crises. Having one office that can adapt agreements and communicate changes to all programs, departments, colleges, and host sites ensures continuity. We saw examples of this during the COVID-19 pandemic, when internship programs had to adapt their agreements to ensure student safety, particularly for persisting face-to-face internships.

Outreach to community organizations to serve as host sites represents another good candidate for centralization (see Chapter 4 for additional discussion of this topic from the perspective of developing authentic partnerships with community host sites). When outreach is completely decentralized, campus programs and departments manage outreach and field inquiries from community organizations on their own. This can lead to organizations being inundated with multiple uncoordinated requests from the same university, reinforcing the unfortunate and erroneous impression that our campuses function haphazardly. It can also mean that interested organizations must navigate, on their own, a patchwork of disconnected internship programs and a hierarchical university structure that makes it difficult to determine who to talk to about hosting interns. We know community organizations that finally gave up on hosting campus interns because they could not figure out who to call on campus or were sent to people who dropped the ball. An office that serves as a coordinated entry point for organizations and businesses could funnel interested parties to the right internship programs and departments, ensuring that we are addressing everyone's interests efficiently and professionally.

If centralizing some aspects of internship programming holds so much potential for ensuring student safety, reducing unnecessary redundancy, and facilitating productive partnerships with community organizations, why is there often such resistance to centralization? We suspect at the heart of this resistance is territorialism and fear: fear that we will lose control and decision-making power over the way we craft and implement our internship programs; fear that we will be told that we are violating campus policies and will be reprimanded; fear that the community partnerships that we have spent so much time cultivating will be subsumed under some larger coordinated campus effort, thereby making it difficult for our own students to secure coveted internship placements. In the process of protecting our terrains, we lamentably lose sight of what is best for students.

Addressing the fear and territorialism associated with proposed centralization will require transparency about our intentions and reassurance that departments, colleges, and divisions can retain control over their internship programs. It will also take time as we will need to build trust with staff and faculty and garner buy-in, both of which will be easier if we can demonstrate through actions (rather than simply promises) the benefits of centralizing key internship functions. Supporters and allies (usually early campus adopters of our centralized practices) can be leveraged to bring on board those who are skeptical or who question our intentions as a way to engage the political frame of leadership.

We have seen this work, albeit on a smaller scale, when we developed a college-level internship office in our own College of Liberal Arts and set out to centralize practices like student professional development, the execution of risk and liability MOUs, and community outreach efforts. Many department-level staff and faculty who are responsible for internship programming were not only excited about having access to college-level resources but also relieved to relinquish responsibility for executing risk and liability MOU's. Nevertheless, we had holdouts, department staff and faculty that questioned our intentions as they had experience with other campus initiatives that proved too good to be true. Many of these holdouts came around over time, after we demonstrated that our college-level office had no intention of absorbing all the good work being done at the department level. In some cases, we negotiated compromises to bring departments into the fold, including giving departments time to phase in risk and liability requirements and supporting and honoring the protection of long-standing community partnerships nurtured by departments.

Bolman and Gallos' (2011) leadership frames speak to the work of centralizing key internship tasks like managing risk and liability and outreach to community organizations to host our students. The human resource frame addresses how we will build teams to staff centralized efforts, whereas the structural frame considers the procedures and policies associated with centralization. The symbolic frame calls attention to the importance of developing a shared vision and eliciting buy-in from stakeholders across our campuses. Finally, the political frame considers the potential conflict in centralizing and the need for negotiation and compromise (Bolman & Gallos, 2011).

Faculty and staff workload

Faculty and staff are key to the success of any academic internship initiative. They teach and often design internship courses, creating syllabi and activities that align with the key elements of high-quality HIPs (e.g., self-reflection, connection of coursework to real-world scenarios, etc.) (Kuh & O'Donnell, 2013). They help students find internship placements, create safe spaces for students to share their internship experiences, cultivate and maintain relationships with host sites, and resolve site challenges. While it is ultimately up to students to determine their deliberate learning objectives, faculty and internship program staff play a crucial role in this process by encouraging students to think about the skills and knowledge they want to acquire and master during the internship period. Faculty and staff also navigate campus policies including those that govern risk and liability and assess the impact of internship programming. In short, faculty and staff wear many hats inside and outside the classroom: instructor, trainer, mentor, problem-solver, cheerleader, and advocate.

It is, therefore, necessary to address head on who specifically is doing this work—which faculty and staff—and how we recognize their efforts, compensate their work, and provide critical training. In short, a successful internship initiative, one that embraces equitable practices, will have committed serious time to addressing the human resource aspects. Unfortunately, we have found that the essential work to create internship opportunities for students is often devalued, siloed, and feminized. After all, this is rarely the sort of work that is factored into promotion or long-term contracts. It is ironic; we value the act of completing internships for students in that they confer many benefits to those who complete them, yet we do not value the labor spent placing students at organizations or building authentic partnerships with host sites. But why? Hatton (2017) contends that we devalue work like that of developing internship opportunities because there is a "naturalization of skill phenomenon in which (some) workers' skills and abilities are construed *not* as products of their hard work, talent, and expertise but as their natural way of being" (p. 340). This happens especially when women shoulder much of the responsibility for overseeing internship programming. Even when women are seen as skilled and capable, they carry an extra burden, unlike their men counterparts, of being innately caring. Women working with community organizations or working closely with students to address barriers to internship participation can be devalued as such workers are allegedly doing "what comes naturally" by virtue of their gender.

When the work to implement internship programs is undervalued, it becomes invisible or siloed (much like unpaid internship placements) by default—out of sight of the larger academic mechanisms and those who have the power to elevate that work to a level of importance (Hatton, 2017). In many cases, this work (frequently unpaid) is literally out of sight, as much of it occurs during summer months and holiday breaks, before academic semesters/quarters begin. The timing of this work can be particularly detrimental to tenure track faculty who are on nine-month contracts and who often choose to work on their own scholarly, creative, or personal endeavors during summers and holiday breaks.

Some may suggest delegating or deferring this work entirely to staff and part time faculty. However, when the responsibility for organizing and overseeing internship programming falls to precarious workers including temporary staff and lecturers, it only serves to further isolate and devalue the labor of internship production (O'Keefe & Courtois, 2019). Several lecturers we talked to (all women) who oversee large internship programs described what can only be labeled as exploitative and unethical. These women are cultivating community partnerships, helping students locate site placements, and managing complicated online platforms for tracking student hours and conducting assessments, all without compensation or acknowledgement. "I feel taken advantage of; it's abusive," is a sentiment we heard repeatedly. When they asked for course release time or a stipend for completing this work, lecturers were told that there are "no funds to support the coordination of internship programming" and that it is "just part of teaching internship courses." Not surprisingly, the only ones teaching internship courses in these circumstances were lecturers. In departments where tenure track faculty teach internship courses, there seemed to be a somewhat greater appetite for providing compensation for internship coordination, although in some situations even tenure track faculty are "volun-told" that they need to shoulder this work without compensation. Lecturers were further given ultimatums: that if they did not want to do the work to coordinate internship programming, they could opt out of teaching the internship courses. Unfortunately, the lecturers in question, and lecturers in general, do not have the luxury of opting out, as they need the internship classes to fill out their employment contracts. Further, they feared that opting out would be tantamount to making public statements about the treatment they were receiving and that could jeopardize their employment altogether. We have cause to be concerned that the situation will worsen given the impassable barriers between those who have the power to make decisions about resources and awards, on the one hand, and the growing numbers of marginalized, invisible workers who are doing the internship housework of the academy, on the other hand.

How can we reconcile these shortcomings and move towards more equitable and fair internship staffing practices? Clearly the first step is to compensate faculty and staff who are already shouldering much of this work during the academic year, holiday breaks, and summer months. But that is not enough. In most cases, additional staff and faculty will be needed if we are to sustain and scale equitable internship programming. Relying on one person to oversee university internship programming is dangerous, even if the person is compensated fairly. What happens if (or when) that person leaves the university? All the program knowledge they built and their relationships with campus and community partners could be jeopardized or lost, making it difficult to sustain university-wide internship efforts. We have seen good internship programs dissolve, wither, or crumble because they were built on the back of one person. Like other parts of internship anatomy we have discussed to this point, infrastructure is key.

A better strategy is one that accounts for and welcomes growth, such as a stepped staffing approach whereby dedicated staff positions are added as internship initiatives evolve. This is the model adopted by the Career Path Internship Program at Idaho State University (n.d.). Initially, one part-time person assisted with the launch of their pilot program. After four years, when it was abundantly clear that the program was successful and would continue, a full-time person was hired. A third full-time staff person was hired recently to focus on outreach efforts in the local (Pocatello) community, as the demand to cultivate more off-campus internship placements for students soared. Instead of overburdening staff and potentially compromising the integrity of their program, Idaho State University (n.d.) recognizes the need to provide adequate staffing. Such a commitment encourages both student and staff success.

We wonder how else to incentivize and reward staff and faculty doing internship work—beyond monetary compensation. For example, could faculty and staff be allowed to co-teach internship courses where they would have the opportunity to collaborate with colleagues and prototype activities and projects? Might we also focus on providing faculty and staff learning communities that create space for deeper conversations (Finely et al., 2022) and ongoing professional development opportunities (not just one-offs) that would not only enhance the current work they are doing but also serve as marketable skills for future jobs? Finely et al. (2022) argue that professional development for those leading HIPs like internships must be "proactive, practical, and inclusive . . . and should tackle issues like implicit bias, discrimination, students' cognitive development, and the learning process itself" (p. 23). At our university, we provide a range of training for faculty who teach internship courses and staff who run internship programs, including paraprofessional certifications like Mental Health First Aid. One of our internship instructors notes:

> As a Psychology professor who has worked in the crisis intervention field, I was initially concerned that I wouldn't get much out of the mental health first aid training. I couldn't have been more wrong! The training went well beyond basic crisis intervention techniques and really gave us an opportunity to think about and discuss professionally relevant and often subtle examples. I also really enjoyed the discussions about the video vignettes. Responding to actual scenarios helped us identify warning signs, and our subsequent group discussions helped us come up with a variety of appropriate responses that we might not have thought of on our own. This ended up being quite useful, as I had a student disclose mental health issues the very next week, and I found myself thinking about everything I learned during the training while I was talking to her . . . I think everyone should take this training. Highly recommend!

Collaborations and coalitions

Myers (2014) defines collaboration as "a process through which parties that see different aspects of a problem can constructively explore their differences and search for solutions that go beyond their limited vision of what is possible" (p. 2). Collaboration is essential for any significant organizational reform, including the creation of institution-wide internship initiatives. Valued internship outcomes that promote equity will require building collaborations and coalitions across campus units and divisions, leveraging talent, and creating a shared vision and culture among those leading internship efforts. Collaborations (just like blended centralization of internship processes) have the potential to eliminate waste and redundancy where services are duplicated across offices and create unnecessary confusion for students. Further, collaborations are all the more important as we experience diminished resources on our campuses and are called upon to do more with less.

True collaborations permeate institutions of higher education both vertically and horizontally and begin with our senior leaders. Presidents, Provosts, and Vice Presidents must not only call for increased collaboration but they must also model collaboration, support collaboration with tangible, sustainable resources, and work to establish an institutional culture that values (even demands) collaboration across divisions. It is time to declare war on siloing and territorialism. After all, the Venn diagram for Academic and Student Affairs has students at its center.

Our research suggests that despite its importance, internship collaboration between divisions, colleges, and programs is scarce in higher education and little institutional incentive to do so exists. At best, we have loose coordination where units are encouraged to exchange information but to "stay in their lane." Staff and faculty do only that which is explicitly in their purview and under their direct control, careful not to step on the toes of those in other units. This coordinated dance, at best characterized as pseudo collaboration, only serves to reproduce and reinforce the silos we have seen historically in internship programming and appears to be especially prevalent in larger public universities where there are more bureaucracies to navigate. Small liberal arts colleges and religious institutions, in contrast, are more likely to be characterized by strong, explicit collaborations (O'Halloran, 2019). Perhaps the former could learn something from the latter and further break down silos across institutions.

As Casciaro et al. (2019) rightfully note, collaborating across boundaries like those between divisions, colleges, and departments are "devilishly difficult" (p. 4). We, too, acknowledge that this is not easy work to accomplish. But we cannot help but (blissfully) imagine what would happen if we prioritized relationship building both vertically and horizontally, if we were willing to come together and engage/collaborate in the name of student success. Before interrogating potential strategies for collaborating, however, we must first address why collaborations are so rare and so difficult to sustain when they are initiated. Although we focus primarily here on collaborations between academic and student affairs as these seem to be the most difficult to navigate, many of our points apply equally to collaborations between departments in the same college and between paid internship programs scattered across the landscape of our campuses. A focus on collaborations between academic and student affairs is further warranted given that for most students, learning experiences (like internships) are neither academic nor cocurricular; they are simply "college."

Arcelus (2011) argues: "The way people define educator can be one of the most significant barriers impeding faculty and student affairs partnerships, and it may be deeply embedded in the cultural norms of both divisions" (p. 65). Faculty in academic affairs tend to focus on the pursuit and dissemination of knowledge both to their disciplinary fields and the students in their classes. To accomplish their work as educators, faculty emphasize the importance of professional autonomy, including academic freedom (O'Halloran, 2019). The culture among faculty, therefore, does not readily value partnerships, but instead prioritizes individuality and hierarchical power. Conversely, staff in student affairs deal with everything outside of the classroom including the overall wellbeing and personal development of students (e.g., student organizations, housing, tutoring, health, career development, basic needs, etc.). O'Halloran (2019) contends that, "the role of student affairs is often viewed as ancillary, supplementary, or complementary to the central academic mission" (p. 303). As a result, student affairs staff may not be seen as co-educators or invited (or welcomed) to the table where serious educational issues are discussed. This role specialization (real or perceived) may also hinder collaborations among staff and faculty in the same division. Faculty often interact more with members of their own discipline in other states and around the world than they do with faculty in other departments or staff across the campus. An administrative position that could unite these two seemingly disparate units might be a Dean or Associate Vice President on what the National Association of Student Personnel Administrators (NASPA) calls a "Common Cause" (O'Brien, 2016).

The fact that we are preoccupied in Higher Education with accountability rather than teamwork can also make collaborations between divisions difficult. It often seems as if we are more concerned with knowing who to blame in case we fail, than to creating the conditions necessary to meet the academic and personal needs of our students. Pisano (2019) makes clear though that "accountability and collaboration can be complementary" (p. 9). Consider a situation where staff in student affairs are responsible for providing student programming for both academic and student affairs internship programs. These staff would collaborate across divisions, seeking input and feedback from a wide range of stakeholders. They would listen to the needs of students and the challenges experienced by student and academic affairs to arrive at a proposed list of training and professional development activities for students which they would be held accountable.

The lack of incentive to collaborate is yet another factor impeding collaborations around internship programming. Institutional rewards and evaluation systems for faculty are traditionally based on research and scholarship productivity, not on collaborations, especially those between divisions. Likewise, performance reviews for those in student affairs rarely highlight cross-division partnerships. If incentives are lacking, why would staff and faculty cooperate or collaborate with people in other divisions if by doing so they are individually worse off? If increased collaboration is a goal, we must ask how we are making it individually useful for people to collaborate. What as leaders are we doing to make it useful and desirable? Just as importantly, what are other, if not all, campus leaders doing to help the cause?

The cornerstone of effective collaboration is a common vision, perhaps in the form of an inclusive strategic planning process and mission, and not in words only. If we are all on the same page and we walk our talk, collaboration comes more naturally. Further, overtly stated common goals and expectations that involve joint implementation and investments break us out of our silos, promote a more authentic sense of ownership, and inform both assessment strategies and resource allocations (Polnariev & Levy, 2016). In short, a well-articulated strategic plan concerning high-impact practices serves as an institution-wide commitment to equitable internship opportunities and a shared approach to making it happen.

For authentic, viable collaborations to occur, for the sake of learning and improving internship opportunities, colleagues must also develop trust and rapport (LePeau, 2015). This is especially important as academic affairs and student affairs often have divergent priorities, allegiances, and perceptions of student success. To build rapport, we need to come together and be willing to ask open-ended questions, consider how others may see the same problem from different angles, and refrain from adopting a bilateral "know it all" approach. We cannot assume we understand what has been said nor should we minimize others' ideas and concerns. Sometimes when we realize we do not know something, we may, out of fear of looking incompetent or weak, dismiss the entire topic. We have seen this in conversations with faculty about the kinds of internships their students are doing and what faculty need in order to better promote and support internships in their own departments. Faculty who never worked outside of academia and/or have no experience in the world of internships have boldly expressed internships are not their responsibility—it is "not their job" to worry about whether and how to secure internships for their students—that is the job of student affairs (e.g., the Career Center) or college-level internship offices. We believe this devaluing and deferring of internships and any collaborative efforts with student affairs is not about a lack of interest but instead a manifestation of a deep-seated fear some faculty have that any investment our university makes in vocational training (workforce development) or post-graduation job placement will erode their value, perhaps even render them obsolete.

One drastic way to break down internship silos and to encourage collaboration is to collapse student and academic affairs into one division or shift programs and units to other divisions. "But that approach has limits: It's costly, confusing, and slow. Worse, every new structure solves some problems but creates others" (Casciaro et al., 2019, p. 132). Short of reorganizing our institutional infrastructures, we might instead focus on facilitating boundary crossing so that staff and faculty in different divisions, units, programs, and departments can connect with the expertise they need to implement high-quality internship programs and placements.

What, then, might facilitate boundary crossing? We rely here on the work of Casciaro et al. (2019) to guide our thinking. They contend that one way to facilitate it is to capitalize on the informal roles that people already occupy such as that of *cultural broker*—those who have demonstrated the ability to forge and nurture collaborations across units and divisions. Cultural brokers have cultivated relationships that span multiple departments and divisions and thus can adeptly connect them. Casciaro et al. (2019) propose that:

> These cultural brokers promote cross-boundary work in one of two ways: by acting as a *bridge* or as an *adhesive* . . . A bridge offers himself as a go-between, allowing people in different functions or geographies to collaborate with minimal disruption to their day-to-day routine. Bridges are most effective when they have considerable knowledge of both sides and can figure out what each one needs.
>
> (p. 133)

This type of cultural brokering is economical as it does not require either collaborating division or department to change what they are doing or address any differences in mission or goals. The problem here is that collaboration between divisions and departments hinges on a single person and their skills. As was noted previously, building initiatives on the backs of single individuals is dangerous as programs and collaborations have a tendency to fall apart when that individual moves on to another position. To sustain institutional innovation over the long term, it is important to develop structural collaborations that transcend the hustle of a few passionate faculty or staff. Casciaro et al. (2019) champion the use of adhesives who:

> in contrast, bring people together and help build mutual understanding and lasting relationships . . . Adhesives facilitate collaboration by vouching for people and helping them decipher one another's language. Unlike bridges, adhesives develop others' capacity to work across a boundary in the future without their assistance.
>
> (p. 133)

Relying on adhesives rather than bridges may be a better long-term strategy for building collaborations across student and academic affairs, as adhesives can step away from the collaboration after initial connections are made without the alliance falling apart. The downside to this strategy is that it requires more time and the ability to hire people with strong interpersonal skills, multicultural competencies, inquisitiveness, humility, and the ability to lead with empathy. We do not prioritize these qualities when hiring faculty; instead, we look for people who have established expertise in their disciplines, the "shiny objects" who have long publication and grant track records. Perhaps moving forward our interview protocol ought to include questions that tap the ability to collaborate.

The Career Path Internship Program at Idaho State University (n.d.) offers us an example of what successfully collaborating across academic and student affairs might look like. The program is managed in the Career Center in student affairs, but faculty in academic departments play a central role. Specifically, faculty submit proposals to the program, requesting funds to pay students for their work at their internship sites. Program staff review proposals annually and make decisions about which academic departments will receive funding (and how much), and then facilitate placements by processing all risk and liability agreements with off-campus sites and conducting assessments of students' experiences. Faculty in academic departments work directly with students and the host sites to ensure mutually beneficial placements and the meeting of learning goals. We would characterize this cross-division collaboration as one that is fostered by program staff who serve as adhesives in that they bring together people across divisions, promote lasting relationships, and help faculty develop the skills necessary to advocate for internship funding from the program and support interns at their placement sites. The collaboration does not hinge on the presence of one specific individual and thus has been sustained for more than a dozen years (Idaho State University, n.d.).

A discussion about collaborations would be incomplete without recognizing the potential value of cultivating relationships with organizations and people outside our universities. Perhaps organizations like the American Association of Colleges and Universities (AACU) and the National Association of Student Personnel Administrators (NASPA) can provide legitimacy and safe spaces for us to explore our ideas and brainstorm about how to push internship initiatives forward on our campuses. A few years ago, we took a team of staff and faculty drawn from both academic and student affairs to the Institute on High-Impact Practices and Student Success held by AACU. Our goal in participating was to develop an action plan for prioritizing collaborations and creating institutional infrastructures that allow for the centralization of HIPs assessment and tracking, execution of risk and liability, and community outreach. At the Institute, we consulted with experts, brainstormed ideas, and committed to collaborating across divisions. Our resulting action plan was the first draft of a successful proposal to our campus senior leadership for the formation of an Academic Internships Office housed in academic affairs with strong ties to our Career Development Center housed in student affairs.

Funding streams

Committing resources for infrastructural support including staff lines and faculty stipends/course buyout are necessary but not sufficient for ensuring equitable access to and participation in internships, especially for our most vulnerable students. We argue that universities must also prioritize, and fund paid internship opportunities. While Chapter 3 discusses the EDIA reasons for prioritizing paid internships, here we focus on the funding streams necessary for offering these paid opportunities. Where will funds come from to offer paid internships to students? And whose responsibility is it to raise the necessary funds? There is likely no single or best approach to funding paid internships. Instead, university size, geographic location, and the willingness of senior administrators to participate in fundraising will determine the best approach for each university.

The Career Path Internship Program at Idaho State University (n.d.) provides a solid example of what can be done when the university President champions paid internships and includes them in their general budget as a line item. As noted previously, the program began with an investment from the campus President of $250,000. Now in its 12th year, ISU pays internship wages annually for upwards of 1,000 students (undergraduate and graduate) completing on- and -off-campus career- and major-related internships. The initial monetary investment (and pilot program) has grown over the years and now tops $2 million annually with three-quarters of that funding coming from the general campus budget. The remaining $500,000 comes from funding by the Idaho state legislature, who has taken notice of the program and the benefits to both students and the local workforce. These investments in offsetting the costs associated with paid internship programs mean that staff do not have to fundraise and can instead devote their time to the selection and support of student interns. It also means that staff can plan for the future without wondering about the status of funds to support paid interns (Idaho State University, n.d.).

In the absence of a budget commitment from senior administrators to fund paid internships, some universities are leveraging longstanding university donors (individuals and organizations) interested in diversifying the local workforce and/or supporting students' post-graduation success. We on our campus, for example, have been successful in lobbying individual donors who are committed to local students returning to their own neighborhoods after graduation to work and live. These donors have given money to support students completing semester-long internships with local non-profit organizations and small businesses. As a direct result of completing these internships, over 50% of student interns receive job offers either from their internship sites or from someone they were able to network with during their internship placements. The success of this paid internship program has spawned similar internship initiatives on our campus that serves students with disabilities, undocumented students, and students interested in social-justice work.

Targeting individuals and businesses capable of funding paid internship placements requires a keen understanding of key players in a university's funding terrain and their specific interests and agendas (political frame). What is of interest to one funder may not be of interest to others. For example, we have encountered potential donors with very specific interests, often based on their own previous experiences—a former college volleyball player who wants to support internships for athletes, and a woman whose daughter struggled with dyslexia in college interested in funding internship scholarships for students with disabilities. Here again is where having cross-division collaborations and the support of key administrators plays a critical role. Faculty and staff running internship programs are unlikely to have access to information about potential donors (nor the political power) necessary for launching effective fundraising campaigns. This type of information and leveraging power comes from Presidents and Development Officers often housed in colleges, advancement, or university-relations offices. While it is the job of Development Officers, among other things, to solicit gifts and support fundraising activities, they may not be tasked with soliciting gifts to support internships or have any direct contact with staff and faculty who run internship programs.

An alternative to soliciting donations from individuals or businesses is to seek grant funding from foundations and governmental agencies. Once again, there is the issue of who will do the legwork to secure this funding. Internship staff and faculty may not have the necessary grant-writing expertise or time to complete grant proposals. In these instances, having access to dedicated grant writers on campus who are knowledgeable about local, state, and national grant opportunities will be necessary.

A recent illustration of using government funding to support paid internships is the #CaliforniansForAll College Corps Program (California Volunteers Office of the Governor, 2023) that began in 2022. This statewide program funded by approximately $300 million in state money has three goals: (1) create a generation of civic-minded leaders with the ability to bridge divides and solve problems; (2) help low-income students graduate college on time and with less debt; and (3) address societal challenges and help build more equitable communities across California. In the first year of the program, 45 campuses (4-year universities and community colleges) across the state have recruited over 3,200 students and have placed them with community non-profit organizations and K-12 schools. Sixty-eight percent are Pell Grant eligible, 64% are first-generation college students, and over 80% are students of color. Over the course of the academic year, students complete 450 hours of service—addressing problems in the state including K-12 education gaps, food insecurity, and climate change. The first cohort of 3,200 students includes more than 500 California Dream Act students, who came to the United States as undocumented immigrants but otherwise qualify for in-state tuition in California. Typically, undocumented students cannot participate in national service programs because federal rules prohibit them from receiving funding. For their service, students receive both a monthly living allowance and an education award totaling $10,000 (California Volunteers Office of the Governor, 2023).

Several universities that received College Corp funding, including our campus, have leveraged the funding and flexible program structure to envision the required service hours as paid internships for junior- and senior-level undergraduates. Students accepted into the program interview with community non-profit organizations to determine their placements and then enroll in and complete an internship course during the first semester of their placements. In addition to gaining real-world job experience, students engage in professional development training and networking with community professionals.

A challenge to relying on donations and grants to fund paid internship programs can include student eligibility criteria dictated by donors that conflict with your program's mission. We have had interested donors insist on a GPA requirement (3.5 out of 4.0) despite our stated interest in recruiting students who show great potential but who have traditionally been excluded from paid internship opportunities due to lack of experience or lower GPAs. Likewise, we have had interested donors (individuals and granting agencies) insist that we restrict their gift/funds to supporting students who are US citizens despite our focus on inclusivity and commitment to providing internship opportunities for undocumented students. In short, you might find yourself in situations where you must decide whether to compromise your mission or principled values to secure funding.

One additional limitation of relying on fundraising efforts that target private donors, foundations, and governmental agencies is the time-limited nature of this funding. A few grants or donations extend beyond a year and thus must be renewed or new funding streams identified. This can lead to a never-ending quest for the next funding source and destabilization of internship programming. Given these challenges, we encourage innovative strategies for funding paid internship placements. Florida State University provides an example of what can be done when we think creatively; they include paid internships as part of major contracts with companies that do business with the university:

> For instance, new Coca-Cola and Sodexo contracts for beverage and food supply included several paid internships as part of the contracts. The inclusion of internships signaled an institutional priority; doing business with the university meant playing a role in educating the next generation of talent.
>
> (O'Shea et al., 2022, p. 194)

Expecting companies that do business with the university to host paid interns not only increases funding for these placements and builds a pipeline of talent for organizations (discussed in more detail in Chapter 5) but it is also an opportunity for the university to walk its talk (McNair et al., 2020).

Policies and procedures

The final piece of institutional infrastructure necessary for ensuring equitable access to academic internships is the campus policies and procedures that govern internship programming. In many cases, our longstanding and well-intentioned policies inadvertently continue to disadvantage our most vulnerable students. That is, there is little institutional alignment of processes and practices with our stated goals of equitable access to internships. For example, to be eligible to receive a stipend, scholarship, or participation award for completing an internship during the semester, students on our campus must be enrolled full-time in coursework which translates to 12 units of credit, typically 4 courses. For many of our students (upwards of 70% according to our most recent assessment surveys), these required course loads translate to a significant barrier or challenge to completing internship hours, especially for students who cannot afford to give up established part-time work (often unrelated to students' long-term educational and career pursuits) for temporary internship placements. There simply are not enough hours in the week for these students to go to class, complete homework, work part- or full-time jobs, and complete internships. Thus, many students (the very ones who have historically been marginalized in terms of internship participation) must opt out of temporary paid internships in their field of study that could provide valuable networking and professional skill development because they must maintain their part- or full-time jobs to pay for rent, tuition, etc. What seems on the surface an answer to equity gaps in internship participation (i.e., paying constituents to complete internships) continues to disadvantage our most vulnerable students.

Relatedly, our policies governing *how* we pay students for completing internships prohibit us from fully addressing equity gaps in internship participation. Many universities require that all stipends, participation awards, and scholarships related to internships be handled and disbursed through Financial Aid Offices. This means that students must have "unmet financial need" as calculated by Financial Aid to receive the stipend or payment as cash. When students do not have enough room in their financial aid packages to accept the funds, the money either goes to pay off previous loans that would typically come due upon graduation or students forfeit the money. On the face of it, this might not seem problematic as by definition, our low-income students qualify for financial aid and thus should have plenty of room in their financial aid packages to accommodate an internship scholarship or stipend. In reality, many of our students experience what they feel is a zero-sum game. If they accept our scholarship or stipend to complete an internship, they might have to forgo other forms of financial assistance like work-study or merit-based scholarships. Or, they might need to sacrifice the immediate cash benefit of the internship scholarship and apply it to their previous loans. Yes, this helps our students down the line, but it is a difficult conversation to have with a student who cannot pay rent this month or has unavoidable, expensive car repairs. Thinking long-term may be a privilege or luxury our most vulnerable students do not have. In short, what is the incentive to do a paid internship if our institutional structures make it impossible for our low-income students to actually get ahead?

Collaborating with our community partners to pay students for their internship work is rarely the solution to archaic campus policies. Current labor laws make it very difficult for companies and nonprofit organizations to pay students stipends and few of our hosting partners want to make students employees as doing so would trigger a series of paperwork, benefits, and tax challenges for our host sties. Further, when host sites pay student interns wages for their work, students sometimes worry how those payments will negatively affect their ability to qualify for financial aid the next year. While we have not seen creative alternatives to paying students directly, we have heard that some universities are exploring how host sites might pay students' tuition instead in lieu of cash. The obstacle to paying students reminds us that implementing policies and procedures governing academic internships is often a practical endeavor rather than a principled decision even when we include internships in our strategic plans.

This chapter has addressed several components of institutional infrastructure necessary for supporting and scaling equitable internship programming on our campuses: strong senior leadership, centralization of key internship tasks, equitable workloads and compensation for faculty and staff, funding to offset costs of paid internships, collaborations across divisions, and policies and procedures that make it easier (not harder) for students to complete internships and get paid for their work. This sentiment is echoed by Finely et al. (2022): "Institutionalizing HIPs [like internships] with a focus on equity requires the alignment of organizational structures, practices, and resources to broaden access to HIPs, particularly among students who have not previously had access" (p. 21). Creating institutional infrastructure will take time, cost money, and require attention to all four leadership frames: human resource, structural, symbolic, and political (Bolman & Gallos, 2011).

References

Arcelus, V. J. (2011). If student affairs-academic affairs collaboration is such a good idea, why are there so few examples of these partnerships in American Higher Education? In P. M. Magolda & M. B. Baxter Magolda (Eds.), *Contested issues in student affairs: Diverse perspectives and respectful dialogue* (pp. 61–74). Stylus. https://doi.org/10.4324/9781003443650

Bolman, L. G., & Gallos, J. V. (2011). *Reframing academic leadership.* Jossey-Bass.

Botes, J. (2001). Conflict transformation: A debate over semantics or a crucial shift in the theory and practice of peace and conflict studies. *International Journal of Peace Studies, 8*(2), 1–27. www.jstor.org/stable/41852899

California Volunteers Office of the Governor. (2023). *College corps.* https://www.californiavolunteers.ca.gov/californiansforall-college-corps-for-college-students/

Casciaro, T., Edmondson, A. C., & Jang, S. (2019). Cross-silo leadership: How to create more value by connecting experts from inside and outside the organization. *Harvard Business Review, 97*(3), 130–139. https://hbr.org/2019/05/cross-silo-leadership

CSULB University Strategic Communications. (2021). *Beach 2030: A roadmap for the next decade.* California State University, Long Beach.

Finely, A., McNair, R., & Clayton-Pedersen, A. (2022). Designing equity-centered high-impact practices. In J. Zilvinskis, J. Kinzie, J. Daday, K. O'Donnell, & C. Vande Zande (Eds.), *Delivering on the promise of high-impact practices: Research and models for achieving equity, fidelity, impact, and scale* (pp. 17–29). Stylus.

Hatton, E. (2017). Mechanisms of invisibility: Rethinking the concept of invisible work. *Work, Employment & Society, 31*(2), 336–351. www.jstor.org/stable/26500194

Idaho State University. (n.d.). *Career Path Internship (CPI) program.* www.isu.edu/career/cpi-program/

Interaction Design Foundation. (n.d.). *Design thinking. What is design thinking?* IxDF. interaction-design.org

Kuh, G., & O'Donnell, K. (2013). *Ensuring quality & taking high-impact practices to scale.* Association of American Colleges & Universities [AAC&U]. aacu.org

Langemak, L. (2022, December 6). Same tools, new use: What if we rethink the internship? *Inside Higher Ed.* Eight what-if questions for colleges to ask about internships (opinion). insidehighered.com

LePeau, L. (2015). A grounded theory of academic affairs and student affairs partnerships for diversity and inclusion aims. *The Review of Higher Education, 39*(1), 97–122. https://doi.org/10.1353/rhe.2015.0044

McNair, T. B., Bensimon, E. M., & Malcom-Piqueux, L. (2020). *From equity talk to equity walk: Expanding practitioner knowledge for racial justice in higher education.* Jossey-Bass.

Merriam-Webster. (n.d.). Gadfly. *Merriam-Webster.com Dictionary.* Retrieved July 19, 2023, from www.merriam-webster.com

Myers, S. (2014). *Enhancing collaboration by examining faculty and student affairs professionals through an intercultural lens.* American College Personnel Association.

O'Brien, P. (2016, January 25). *Partnering student affairs and academic affairs: Collaboration for a common cause.* National Association of Student Personnel Administrators. naspa.org

O'Halloran, K. C. (2019). A classification of collaboration between student and academic affairs. *College Student Journal, 53*(3), 301–314.

O'Keefe, T., & Courtois, A. (2019). 'Not one of the family': Gender and precarious work in the neoliberal university. *Gender, Work, and Organization, 26*(4), 463–479. https://doi.org/10.1111/gwao.12468

O'Shea, J., Hoover, M., & Hunt, J. (2022). Increasing student access and learning in employment and internship experiences. In J. Zilvinskis, J. Kinzie, J. Daday, K. O'Donnell, & C. Vande Zande (Eds.), *Delivering on the promise of high-impact practices: Research and models for achieving equity, fidelity, impact, and scale* (pp. 188–198). Stylus.

Pisano, G. P. (2019). The hard truth about innovative cultures. *Harvard Business Review, 97*(1), 62–77. https://hbr.org/2019/01/the-hard-truth-about-innovative-cultures

Polnariev, B. A., & Levy, M. A. (2016). Promoting student success via collaboration. In M. A. Levey & B. A. Polnariev (Eds.), *Academic and student affairs in collaboration: Creating a culture of student success* (pp. 1–20). Routledge.

Princeton Review. (2023). Best value colleges. https://www.princetonreview.com/college-rankings/best-value-colleges

3 Intersequity, Students of Color, and the Perils of Unpaid Internships

Scholarship on equity issues facing college internships is rich, yet discipline- and institution-specific findings often render it restrictive by default. Likewise, literature reviews, although valuable resources for understanding the critical landscape, are incompatible with provocative praxis. This chapter thus draws broader attention and takes sweeping approaches to inequities as they interface with Students of Color intersectionality. As Hora et al. (2020) assert, "few studies have examined the nature of specific barriers to internship participation, particularly with respect to low-income, first-generation, and/or minoritized college students" (p. 236). Leading with race and incorporating adjacent forms of self-identification that can aggravate oppression helps in understanding and addressing the "whole student." While we would be hard pressed to ruminate on every possible intersectional identity combination, engaging in provocative praxis contextually can help expose and consequentially minimize barriers-to-internships issues. As McNair et al. (2020) assert: "an honest assessment of, and genuine reckoning with, the structural barriers and hidden biases that pervade our own colleges, universities, organizations and associations, mitigating against articulated equity goals as the foundation for student success" (p. xvi). Similarly, we acknowledge invisibility in this assessment, what Perlin (2011) calls "the non-interns," those students who never pursue one, and why those who do must be accounted for, both as subject non-participants and as data point exclusions (p. 160).

Our case study for this chapter comes from our own, Southern-California backyard: The Long Beach Community Internship Project (LBCIP, n.d.), under the auspices of faculty and staff at California State University, Long Beach. LBCIP, which launched in spring 2021, is a goal-oriented initiative and the only campus internship program that recruits, places, and mentors student interns across all seven colleges. While intended for all Long Beach Promise Students (LBP)—that is, Long Beach Unified School District-hailing students—it strives to increase paid internship opportunities for traditionally underrepresented groups such as Students of Color, first-generation, and Pell-eligible individuals. To date, 95% of LBCIP participants are Students of Color, and 80% will be the first in their families to earn a college degree. Born from a

DOI: 10.4324/9781003296324-3

desire to create opportunities for students to do meaningful work in their own neighborhoods, including that which promotes social justice, LBCIP allows LBP students to, "apply coursework to real-world settings, hone professional skills, network, and explore local career opportunities" (para. 2). Establishing collaborations with regional non-profits, city departments, and small businesses creates a pipeline of talent, a critical component of California State University, Long Beach's commitment to advancing partnerships for the public good. Indeed, for more than a third of the 60-some Long Beach non-profits hosting LBCIP students, this is their first-ever connection or collaboration with California State University, Long Beach. This aligns with California State University, Long Beach's commitment to advancing commonwealth partnerships that are a boon for all involved, thereby, as per the LBCIP landing page, "creating a bridge for students back to their communities to work, live, and thrive" (Long Beach Community Internship Program, n.d., para. 3).

With this model in mind, the intersectionality of this chapter's own intersectional scaffolding—where Students of Color, intersequity, and data meet—allows for multi-directional provocation at critical points of convergence. Despite the inevitable overlap inherent to these topics, we trust that any repetition henceforward serves to reinforce claims, underscore the strategies involved, and expose the inequities therein. It is in this way that we move toward authentic, sustainable student success.

Students of Color

Alison Doyle (2022) reports that our Students of Color are underserved where internships are concerned: "only 59.5% of Black students and 53.3% of Latinx students participate in internships, compared to 68.2% of White students" (para. 2). Yosso (2005) gives further nuance to these statistics: "Indeed, racism and its intersections with other forms of subordination shape the experiences of People of Color very differently than Whites" (p. 73). Because documenting differential access and experiences of internships does not address the why, everyone stands to gain in accounting for a range of barriers—including campus internship policies and practices in conjunction with a student's cultural and identity affiliations—that might prevent certain groups of students from enrolling in an internship. As Hora et al. (2021) assert, "Research demonstrates that a 'one-size-fits-all' approach to teaching and learning, student affairs, and career development ignores both historic and structural inequalities while also overlooking the unique needs, circumstances, and potentials of a diverse student body" (p. 2). These circumstances include pandemic stressors, from students whose internships were rendered moot to those who pivoted to online internships to those who persisted despite the health risks involved. Indeed, COVID-19 exacerbated myriad inequities. In fleshing out these challenges, provocative praxis reorients the narrative we have enabled and perpetuated regarding internship participation and non-participation.

Students of Color who pursue internships are at a disadvantage (by default), as Hora et al. (2021) highlight: "the racial discrimination that racially minoritized students may face in securing an internship is often compounded by longstanding social arrangements that privilege students who have access to financial, social, and cultural capital" (p. 13). Similarly, Hora's (2022a) College Internship study exemplifies the consequences of being less than privileged. According to the survey and focus group findings, which included three HBACUs, students identified barriers that corroborate realities: 63% could not give up their current, paying job; 60% cited heavy course load; 37% blamed insufficient internship pay; 26% bemoaned lack of transportation; and 16% lacked childcare (Hora, 2022, pp. 115–116). This regrettably, albeit compellingly, aligns with the findings from Kinzie, Silberstein, et al. (2021), who confirm,

> Expectations about time was a common theme across racially minoritized students' responses, particularly when it came to the least satisfying aspect of their HIP experience. Racially minoritized students highlight how they were required to balance multiple projects and obligations simultaneously. As one Latinx student doing service-learning shared, "[A]ll the work I had to put into it, a full-time job, full-time school, kids and a project is hard to balance." A multiracial senior in a culminating experience commented, "[T]he amount of time consumed by the project is almost overwhelming, especially when compared with the time required for all other coursework."
>
> (p. 10)

Despite the cited stressors, students' comments nevertheless recall Yosso's (2005) concept of navigational capital, the ability of racially minoritized students to navigate in learning environments, even when these spaces may be unwelcoming or unsupportive. Imagine the outcomes, then, if more of those spaces were rendered hospitable! Such a shift begins with adopting a strengths-forward, empathy-leading mentality—recognition, appreciation, flexibility, and willingness to pivot—to inform student learning and success. The human resources frame can help faculty and the students they serve benefit from championing the latter's cultural assets by "caring for individuals and supporting their growth and development" (Bolman & Gallos, 2011, p. 100). Whether a course enrolls students by major, internship type, or college (or any other enrollment-based criteria), it ought to ultimately make the student intern worry less about juggling responsibilities and think more about their place within the internship as well as the world. This is just one way that faculty can deliver on the commitment to mutualism (see Chapter 1).

Indeed, these challenges are surmountable if we as leaders acknowledge and reframe them. Cia Verschelden's (2017) *Bandwidth Recovery: Helping Students Reclaim Cognitive Resources Lost to Poverty, Racism and Social*

Marginalization is a useful starting point when rethinking equity vis-à-vis capital, as it reconfigures continuums of income/health/wealth through what she calls a strengths perspective (p. xiv), which aligns with Yosso's (2005) community cultural wealth model. Culture, which she defines as "frequently represented symbolically through language and can encompass identities around immigration status, gender, phenotype, sexuality and region, as well as race and ethnicity," is what ultimately determines one's wealth (Yosso, 2005, p. 76). Cultural capital subsumes meeting—and valuing—students where they are and upends deficit thinking.

This perspective, as opposed to its deficiency-perspective counterpart (i.e., what students lack), instead celebrates students' "funds of knowledge" and underscores the importance of "recovering mental bandwidth" (Verschelden, 2017, p. xiv). As the author explains, "Bandwidth refers to the cognitive and emotional resources needed to deal with making good decisions, learning, caring for family, having healthy relationships, and more" (p. xiii). Verschelden's (2017) book forces us to interrogate our own assumptions and deficit thinking that place the cause (blame) for inadequate participation or performance on students. If, for instance, a student is a primary caregiver in their extended family, has additional childcare responsibilities, works more than part-time to support the household, and is enrolled full-time at their university, is there realistically room for an internship? One step toward reconciliation might be to apply the strengths perspective to bring the internship in line with students' lives and priorities rather than strongarm them into alignment with the internship: finding the dorm-living student an internship on campus, securing an internship that informs or is informed by their cultural capital, or converting the student's current job into an internship.

The human resource and symbolic frames provide the scaffolding for transformative action in internship contexts (Bolman & Gallos, 2011). By this, we mean "Establishing a culture of equity-mindedness [that] depends greatly on leaders who go beyond rhetorical praise for diversity, inclusiveness, and equity. It requires leaders who model the tenets of equity-mindedness in language and action" (McNair et al., 2020, p. 49). While some may question the workload implications inherent to "action," we defer to campus leadership, whose responsibility is to provide the resources for deep work, in both quantity and quality, to transpire. McNair et al. (2020) refer to this as "engaged inclusivity," whereby as students actively pursue their educational goals, the institution must do its part by "creating a learning environment that promotes equity and inclusion by understanding the diversity of the students that it seeks to educate" (p. 4). Work suddenly becomes manageable and sustainable—if not rewarding—when it is first perceived as valuable and supported, both fiscally and symbolically, by administrators, a topic discussed fully in Chapter 2. This is when capitalization on student initiative, from a strength's perspective, only becomes possible. By leaning into these perspectives— reframing Students of Color's social capital and acknowledging the skills, experiences, willingness, and wisdom that they bring to campus—provocative praxis enables us to adopt a symbiotic model of learning that pervades *InternsHIPs*.

Even when we feel we are, in fact, in tune with our internship-taking or seeking Students of Color, provocative praxis is most useful as an ongoing, preventative practice. For example, existing data indicate that Students of Color completing internships are more likely to engage with diverse ideas and ways of thinking (Rojas et al., 2021). Is this, then, a conferred benefit or more of a burdensome expectation, an outgrowth from racism and classism? In the provocative spirit, we wonder why Students of Color may be more likely than their white peers to do the work to understand diverse points of view and why, by default, they are singled out (because of their race) to develop these new ways of thinking. One answer suggests that Students of Color experience racism and classism at their internship sites (i.e., microaggressions) that imply that their views and backgrounds—and by association, themselves—are somehow not compatible with their chosen career settings. An additional problematic upshot involves interns becoming the "face" of their cultural identity. For instance, Students of Color interns may encounter stereotypes (e.g., "Asians are hardworking"), which in turn impacts their behavior and expectations to increase mental—and by association, "work"—loads.

LBCIP is proof that the best, sustainable, most equitable solutions are always informed by and realized through provocative praxis. Over a hundred LBCIP student interns (mostly of Color) amassed over 10,000 internship hours, contributing over $333,000 of labor to (stimulate) the local Long Beach economy (Long Beach Community Internship Program, n.d.). Student Field Placement Agreements are now in place with all non-profit partners, ensuring Risk Management policy compliance. And exit surveys indicate the endeavor's transformative impact. As one intern noted,

> The LBCIP has been nothing short of a positive experience and has paved the way and opened doors that I didn't know existed. I'm walking away with inspiration, a new perspective on my professional career, and gratitude for having the pleasure to work with wonderful people.

The program is a testament to our Students of Color's potential under the right conditions.

Notwithstanding, bringing LBCIP to fruition was an arduous enterprise, having essentially rested (and still resting) on the shoulders of one campus individual. Even with the ability to engage all leadership frames to secure buy-in, hire the right people, and publicly promote the local program, resourcing and overseeing the program puts a strain on workload and sustainability (see Chapter 2). Authentic EDIA action would imply line-item financial support that is guaranteed each semester to pay for the administrative costs; paid, dedicated staff/faculty, a director focused on the development and fundraising to sustain the program and to do the work associated with running the program; and greater symbolic support of the program through highlighting in campus publications, website, events, and community events. Ultimately, campus leadership will determine the fate of LBCIP in the years to come and will have to engage in and contend with more provocative praxis, as the success of the program, and that of our Students of Color, continues.

Intersequity: intersectionality meets equity

Kimberlé Crenshaw brought the now-ubiquitous, political term "intersectionality" into being in 1989 and was asked in Katy Steinmetz's 2020 *Time* interview for an updated definition in the post-Trump era:

> It's basically a lens, a prism, for seeing the way in which various forms of inequality often operate together and exacerbate each other. We tend to talk about race inequality as separate from inequality based on gender, class, sexuality or immigrant status. What's often missing is how some people are subject to all of these, and the experience is not just the sum of its parts.
>
> (p. 140)

While intersectionality infers (in)equality, as per Crenshaw's statement, advancing toward equity requires provocative praxis (Steinmetz, 2020). Moncada (2017) grounds the term, as it relates to People of Color interns, it in its own absence: "Equity is feeling welcomed and empowered to join a field that is not diverse" (p. 5). While some college internships—inclusive of the programs that sponsor them—model best EDIA practices, countless others flounder. When they do, those who are most negatively impacted are the students they (ironically) intend to serve.

As with Kuh (2008) in Chapter 1 ("high-impact practices," p. 9), dilating concepts and ideas is part of provocative praxis. In the context of internships, intersequity implies intersectional justice, which aims to identify as well as reconcile inequities, as per those implicated in the Black Lives Matter movement: "Black queer and trans folks, disabled folks, undocumented folks, folks with records, women, and all Black lives along the gender spectrum. Our network centers those who have been marginalized within Black liberation movements" (Black Lives Matter, n.d., para. 2). We affirm that taking into account the gamut of student-specific statuses and identities (e.g., first-generation, full-or part-time employed, primary caretaking, LGBTQI+, and student-athlete) make for the most equitable practices possible. Indeed, internship equity is as much a human issue as it is a logistical and circumstantial one.

Thijssen and Kessel (2021) see these issues as part of a larger, pervasive, systemic problem, evidenced when they ask urgently, "So, what can be done to help mitigate the effects of this toxic undergraduate internship culture?" (para. 7). The question assumes contradictory, precarious dimensions for our Students of Color, who persist in a paradox: although it has been suggested that the benefits of internships may be greatest for the first-generation students, Students of Color, and those from low-income backgrounds (Freeland Fisher, 2022, para. 1), minoritized students are less likely to participate. To add insult to injury, traditional campus internship practices thwart social mobility (Hora et al., 2019, pp. 25–26). Provocative praxis flourishes in situations that require this type of multi-directional thought processes: "Any thoughtful approach to fixing the current system must proceed along two separate tracks: rectifying the indignities faced by current interns and ensuring greater access to internships that are worthwhile and meet basic criteria of fairness" (Perlin, 2011, p. 207). Provocative praxis strives to rupture silos so that the data paint the most complete—if not compelling—picture possible. Its end goal relates to what McNair et al. (2020) call "sensemaking":

> Equity-minded sensemaking goes beyond examining data and noticing equity gaps in outcomes. It involves interpreting equity gaps as a signal that practices are not working as intended and asking equity minded questions about how and why current practices are failing to serve students experiencing inequities.
>
> (p. 61)

Otherwise, internships remain opportunities exclusively for the privileged (Perlin, 2011).

Equity in the classroom: credit-bearing courses and faculty (mentors)

In full disclosure, this section was originally conceived as a standalone chapter with the word "curriculum" in its title. While such a title might anticipate a discussion of broad academic matters or specific curricular best practices, including faculty training in teaching internship classes and understanding the legalities and policies that govern them—after all, no instructor should be expected to figure it out on their own!—in the spirit of provocative praxis, and to avoid being overly prescriptive, we take a different approach. To that end, this section positions course instructors as creators and gatekeepers of (safe) spaces, particularly for more vulnerable students, who often have fewer of them.

An intern's experience is only as good as their formal and informal evaluations and reporting of it. We might ask ourselves why students fail to advocate on their own behalf when their internship turns sour. This is where (again) an invested advocate plays an important role, as these individuals help emplace and sustain safe spaces for dialogue, strategy, and change. We do not underestimate the conundrum of students' reluctant awareness. Consider, for example, the Latina student (activist) who fears occupational or academic risk; she may worry about repercussions, or, worst-case scenario, fear jeopardizing her internship status. Whether it be a course instructor or staff member, scaffolding ensures agency accountability. At institutions where other subsidies are available to build internship infrastructure, this person could also be a faculty champion, fellow, or confidant. One way to conceptualize the overarching support system for student interns, then, is as a "design team" (Waddoups et al., 2004), with the intern as the "product":

> A design team is a lot like a fashion consultant. The team members are involved in creating a product, reshaping and synthesizing this product, and, in many ways, creating a new fashion. To be a part of a design team means that you design and redesign.
>
> (p. 17)

The team would not only work together to maximize the pedagogical underpinnings of the internship but also the intern's edification as it relates to those underpinnings, including helping them find a voice, negotiate, and advocate for themself. Intercampus teamwork establishes a network of accountability often missing from, if not foreign to, the internship equation. Research shows that students who have good mentors, what Baker and Griffin (2010) label "faculty developers," perform better in college, boast lower attrition rates, and are, by and large, more fulfilled. Tuned-in mentoring is a profound, tangible way to demonstrate that we are, in fact, addressing students' needs and that we work on their behalf, the radical idea underscored in Chapter 1. One to several internship-adjacent mentors may inhabit an intern's academic world and, ideally, would function as do synapses to create a powerful coalition of steering mentorship.

A longstanding, contentious debate regarding internships involves applicable credit and accompanying coursework. Indeed, as few as three decades ago, words such as "legitimacy" beleaguered such courses (Ciofalo, 1988). Today, we see internships without coursework as nullifying the high-impact experience and instead advocate for course credit as part and parcel of any internship (to achieve Benedict and Rust's (2016) "highest-impact" [p. 3]). O'Neill (2010) justifies concurrent internship courses as part of the high-impact confluence:

> We can posit that an internship is more likely be "high impact" for students when it is intentionally organized as an activity that leads to particular

learning outcomes; when students apply what they have learned in courses to work experiences, reflect on these experiences, and receive feedback that helps them to improve.

(p. 5)

The contours of the mentoring relationship between course instructor and intern subsequently deepen through curricular development and consequential, workload-reasonable content.

California State University, Long Beach regularly offers discipline- and major-specific internship courses, particularly in internship-mandated majors, such as Journalism and Public Relations, Speech-Language Pathology, and Human Development. Cognizant that department budgets and allocations vary wildly from year to year, we have developed parallel umbrella courses that can serve any student major within—and theoretically beyond—our second largest college, Liberal Arts. In this way and with a nod to equitable practices, no student is denied the opportunity to intern and/or earn credit for their efforts. Not only does this benefit students by forging a stronger connection between the intern's and the agency's expectations but it also encourages students, in the intellectual spirit of attending college, to ponder individually and collectively the ethics and aims of internships in general.

Since "HIPs are centered in the ideology of Whiteness," according to Kinzie, McCormick, et al. (2021), provocative praxis can serve as a decentering tool to align syllabi and exams, as well as other curricular peripherals, with best equitable practices (para. 10). The co-existence of competing learning modalities, for instance (e.g., in-person vs. online vs. hybrid), entails advantages as well as disadvantages. While an online internship may be convenient for one student (the introvert who lives a distance from their internship and/or lacks transportation), it may hinder another (who learns better through group discussions and struggles to work independently). Freeland Fisher (2022) adds that students deserve to understand how certain choices inform their success. Reconfiguring Kuh's (2008) eight elements in light of Yosso's (2005) cultural capital wealth model, then, ultimately yields what Kinzie, McCormick, et al. (2021) call a threshold for high-quality internships. If we accept the premise by Finley et al. (2023) that "Efforts to examine equity and quality of HIPs should prioritize the process through which educators design learning experiences," broad thinking is necessary (p. 19). While we often talk about EDIA efforts in the context of course content, course delivery—to name one example—should be subject to and part of the decentering process, too. Other recalibrating efforts could involve work-friendly course schedules, low- or no-cost textbooks, and course substitutions.

For years, internship courses have not only been chopping block favorites but also, by and large, have been minimized at the department level (and beyond) when scheduling. Budgetary constraints become at once the justification and the scapegoat. We must, as per O'Neill (2010), address departmental reluctance toward what they see as "vocational education," a misnomer in her eyes, as per her use of the term in quotations (p. 7). This egregious neglect of internship course offerings demonstrates a gross misunderstanding of their impact on the internship experience as well as their relevance as it relates to the term "high impact." It also signals a disregard, if not disdain, for internships in general, which suggests a need for increased internship literacy, beginning with what they are, who they serve (and exclude), what they do, how they do it, and why they matter. As we move beyond the idea that students work at an internship toward one that instead has the internship working for them (our appeal from Chapter 1) as part of internship campaign efforts, we are optimistic that these high-impact practices will soon earn their seat at the university table to inform and be informed by the social-justice leanings of recent, collective, EDIA scholarship.

Unpaid internships: top offender of equity crimes

In this section, we unapologetically, if not vehemently, press for the abolishment of inequity-exacerbating, uncompensated internships, what Perlin (2011) calls "calculated voluntarism" (p. 107). Insight into Diversity (2021) summarizes a survey from Student Loan Hero, which reports that nearly 25% of the United States have worked at some point as an unpaid intern. Other relevant statistics include: 47% assumed new or renewed existing student loans to manage expenses (People of Color respondents were significantly more likely to experience this issue, with 60% indicating they accrued education debt as an intern, compared to their white counterparts [40%]); nearly 55% of respondents believe that these positions give unfair advantages to higher income students who have the luxury to forsake a salary; and 40% of the US Americans think unpaid internships should be abolished because they provide employers with free labor (Insight into Diversity, 2021, para. 2 and 3). Perlin (2011) explains why we might still tolerate unpaid internships:

> Working for free, or even paying to work—a hallmark of many internships—is held to be an innovation of precisely this type: an act of selflessness that also aids a career, a form of barter (labor in exchange for training, contacts, experience, etc.), or a brilliant investment in the future.
>
> (p. 124)

We are encouraged by the National Association of Colleges and Employers' (n.d.-b) position on unpaid internships: "To provide all participating internship students with equitable access to opportunities and career success, we advocate that all internships should be paid" (Unpaid Internships are Problematic section, para. 8).

Hora's (2022b) recent, insightful, albeit sobering yet compelling policy brief, "Unpaid Internships & Inequality: A Review of the Data and

Recommendations for Research, Policy and Practice" further informs the rugged unpaid internship landscape: roughly 30% of all college students complete an internship (though 67% who did not confirm wanting to); the number of unpaid internships ranges from 30.8% to 58.1%; and men are more likely to hold a paid internship (75%) than women and other gender identities (54% and 48%, respectively). While these numbers are a useful starting point, Hora (2022b) laments the limited nature of "robust, cross-institutional data," which ultimately provides only a partial—and thus problematic—view of the internship picture (p. 5).

Such an incomplete image ultimately (and regrettably) disadvantages the students we (most) seek to support and impedes us from understanding myriad issues that impact them. For example, Norman's (2021) piece in Boston's *Berkeley Beacon*, "Internship for credit: gaining experience or getting scammed?," highlights the dual burden of internshipping from a student financial perspective. This amounts to forsaking pay (for their work) and assuming pay (for course credit, often to the tune of several thousands of dollars): "So many internships are already unpaid . . . Colleges should focus on altering their internship costs or partnering with internship placement organizations that employ tuition reimbursement, so students don't have to worry about falling behind" (para. 12). She wonders, as do we, why students at her institution (Emerson College) can receive "up to four credits at no cost to them for their involvement in campus extracurricular activities" yet internships aren't eligible for this same consideration (Norman, 2021, para. 13).

Lest we forget the psychosocial effects of unpaid internships on interns. According to Rothschild and Rothschild (2020): "Generally speaking, research has documented that unpaid interns may report lower levels of satisfaction with their internship experience" (p. 3). Although compensation (or lack thereof) for interns may seem unrelated to pedagogical matters, in fact, financial tribulations often arise and hinder student success. We cannot, therefore, assume that any student can afford to engage in free work when tuition, rent, and basic needs are on the table. When these conditions are unmet, class performance, grades, and mental health suffer and lead to short- and long-term problems.

Perlin's (2011) medical metaphor, "Post-industrial, networked capitalism has provided the ideal petri dish for the growth of internships," hints at an infirm internship industry that hinges, at least in part, on this overabundance of free work (p. 36). Further, as Matthew Hora (2022b) points out, "unpaid internships pose considerable legal, ethical, and practical challenges" (p. 3). In a fair system, such proliferation would be a boon for interns and internships. Currently, however, the imagery implies that not only does free enterprise ensure that the system works for its own benefit but it also does so in a way that perpetuates the malady, as Perlin's (2011) subsequent simile attests: "work that is recognizably work, undertaken without wages in return, is like a virus in the labor force, spreading quickly to other sectors—it should be illegal no matter the net worth of the worker" (p. 165). His comparison underscores the notion that work is work and, therefore, warrants fair compensation.

Perlin (2011) lambastes unpaid internships (and our indifference toward them) as:

> A form of mass exploitation hidden in plain sight. Those who can't afford to work without pay are effectively shut out, while a large group of interns from low- and middle-income backgrounds barely scrapes by. Plum internships are overwhelmingly for the wealthy and well-connected—to an extent that would be shocking if it involved regular jobs. Yet no one budges, nothing happens.
>
> (p. xiv)

A recent study by Phil Gardener (2011) at Intern Bridge quantifies which majors (education and social science students) and groups (women, minorities, and middle-to-low-income students) are more likely to participate in unpaid internship experiences. Gardener (2011) found that unpaid internship participation also was negatively correlated to student salary and employment outcomes (pp. 5–7).

Paid internships, in contrast, provide key advantages for students seeking their first post-college position. Collins (2020) reports via a NACE student survey that paid interns receive more job offers than unpaid interns and more than those who haven't engaged in an internship. In a similar vein, paid interns received an average of 1.12 job offers, unpaid interns received 0.85 offers, and those who had no internship experience received 0.64 offers. In addition, NACE's research consistently shows that those students who had paid internships are also more likely to secure a job prior to graduation. While all types of internships can have value, NACE research has found that paid internships benefit students in their job search in multiple ways, at least in terms of the first job post-graduation: more job offers, higher starting salaries, and a shorter employment search (Collins, 2020).

Even the literary world of fictional interns is rife with evidence of internship inequity and abuse. In *Realities: A Collection of Short Stories* by Teresa Lo (2011), one character, Gabby, who is both sympathetic and relatable, quips to another:

> Unpaid internships are worse than slavery . . . They make us work ridiculous hours, for free, and they make us do things an employee would do. It's a scam, and worse, they make you feel like they're doing YOU a favor. It's such mindfuckery.
>
> (p. 46)

In *This is What I know About Art*, author Kimberly Drew (2020) speaks to her reader directly and from the first-hand experience:

> It's absurd to think about how a $1,600 stipend changed the course of my life. It's absurd to think about how many internships are still unpaid, and how elitist and morally corrupt it is to hire unpaid or underpaid labor.
>
> (p. 15)

We find it telling, if not symptomatic, that both authors are women of color in an example of life-imitating art. Durack (2013) suggests that to remedy this malady, "The most straightforward response, then, would be to require that all internships that are completed for college credit are paid internships that include meaningful work and learning opportunities" (p. 265). Moreover, an unpaid internship that does not qualify has a HIP is doubly (or triply) problematic. Charitybuzz (*charitybuzz.com*), for instance, allows parents, as per the invitation on their landing page, to "bid" on exclusive opportunities for their child to intern at high-profile places or with celebrities. Even if the proceeds benefit charity, low-income students are excluded by default (and those accepted are likely not engaging in a high-impact practice).

It bears repeating that unpaid internships promote and exacerbate inequities. Hora et al. (2020), rightfully point out that "Debates about intern compensation should not solely be limited to their effects on developmental outcomes, but should be steadfastly focused on concerns about equity, fairness and student well-being" (p. 249). Many historically excluded students already work full- and part-time jobs to make ends meet, act as full-time caregivers for family members, and lack the know-how or connections to secure a paid internship. Hora et al. (2020) put the onus on us, which recalls our discussion of mutualism in Chapter 1:

> Ultimately, the field of higher education and WIL [Work Integrated Learning] needs to recognize that while internships may be a vehicle for the transformation of a person from a student to a budding professional, they may also serve to reproduce inequality by making these experiences inaccessible to thousands of students who lack sufficient financial or social capital to locate and pursue these opportunities.
>
> (p. 250)

The legal dimensions of unpaid internships (and loopholes for internship sites) add an additional, latent layer of inequity: "Unpaid internships represent a double injustice—according to legal experts, the lack of pay also mean that these interns have no standing in court as employees, even if they have worked full-time for a year in the same office" (Perlin, 2011, p. 78). Perlin adds, "Those subject to sexual harassment or racial discrimination have no legal recourse" (p. 64). Bowman and Lipp (2000) drive home the implications from a broader legal perspective: "In the eyes of the law, unpaid interns are neither students nor employees; they are invisible" (p. 79). As a result, our Students of Color straddle precarious situations when they work as unpaid interns: "Those subject to sexual harassment or racial discrimination have no legal recourse" (Perlin, 2011, p. 64). Enforcing minimum wage would, as Perlin (2011) rightfully suggests, "bring internships in line with other forms of work" (p. 141).

Unpaid internships not only disadvantage but also take advantage of our Students of Color. Intentional predatory practices aimed at reducing staffing costs are not uncommon. As Perlin (2011) notes, "If well-paid internships more often represent a considered, nuanced investment in talent, unpaid positions may simply be stopgap measures, a way of plugging operational holes" (p. 139). Anecdotally, we know of instances of organizations firing staff because they see the opportunity in being able to rely on an unpaid intern to do business. In the case of parasitic internships (see Chapter 1), the drawbacks for students are directly proportional to the advantages of host sites. Further, if we accept the premise that compensation renders an internship more valuable (to students and future employers), then by deduction, a lack thereof implies frivolity, which, in turn, infers low- or no-impact and can ultimately breed parasitism.

These intersequity issues—including but not limited to race, privilege, compensation, gender—at the junction of unpaid internships and Students of Color implore provocative praxis with the structural frame in mind. In essence, are we the ones (ironically) creating many of the challenges students encounter? Which biases and institutional infrastructures—we have either created or failed to dismantle—support systemic inequities, reinforce privilege, and discriminate against Students of Color as it relates to internships? For example, the traditional approach in many departments for placing students at internship sites is to have them search for placements on their own. We have historically rationalized this practice as "good training" and part of students' "professionalization" for the post-graduation job search. Never do we stop to consider that this swim-or-sink approach reinforces privilege by rewarding those students with larger personal and professional networks and the deeper social capital reserves we have referenced elsewhere in this book. Students with fewer connections rightfully become overwhelmed and either opt into less-than-ideal placements to meet a minimum requirement or opt out completely if the internship course is an elective. Other challenges include GPA minimums, unit counts, and class standings. While these may be important for some students and at certain institutions, waivers and accommodations are great antidotes to inequities. We applaud innovative efforts that disrupt the traditional way of structuring internships and that push the boundaries of feasibility.

Perlin (2011), too, cites societal responsibility for perpetuating unpaid internships and their side effects:

> All of us—employers, parents, schools, government agencies, and interns themselves—are complicit in the devaluing of work, the exacerbation of social inequality and the disillusionment of young people in the workplace that are emerging as a result of the intern boom.
>
> (p. xv)

Reeves' (2017) self-explanatory term "dream hoarding" helps put this continuance into context. He proposes a radical but noble solution to put an end to and to achieve equitable economic progress: stop focusing on bringing down the top 1% and instead raise up those below us (p. 7) or be faced to deal with "meritocracy without mobility" (p. 11). *Dream Hoarders*, in essence, is another reminder of the importance of mutualism and to keep our privilege in check: "Every college place or internship that goes to one of our kids because of a legacy bias or personal connection is one less available to others" (Reeves, 2017, p. 12).

Until dreams are more readily shared, identifying funding sources for unpaid internships remains critical. Edwards et al. (2010) recommend using "federal financial aid to fund public service internships for less affluent students by tapping into the existing Federal Work Study (FWS) to administer internship grants" (p. 6). This would represent not only a practical solution but also an ethical one: "These initiatives would foster opportunity for low-income students, affording them a better chance to compete with their higher-income peers" (p. 6). Assuming that a certain percentage of students may intern in another part of the country, we should also consider other economic challenges, as is the case when students are required to relocate: "Some of the most prestigious unpaid internships are located in expensive cities . . . The University of Dreams, for example, charges $8,000 per person for the guarantee of an eight-week internship with housing in New York City" (pp. 2, 5). The authors add that these types of internships often exclude travel and living expenses (p. 3). In sum, we agree with Edwards et al. (2010) that "Paid internships for lower-income students would represent an important step toward leveling the playing field" (p. 1). The report concludes with a powerful quote from Segal, founder of the youth advocacy organization 80 Million Strong, whose testimony summarizes the unpaid internship dilemma

> [a]t its core, this is an issue of representation. Representative democracy depends on the input, perspective, and experience of all of its citizens, not just the privileged few. If the majority of young America is saddled with debt in order to work pro bono or prevented from the active citizenship experience of serving government because of financial hardship, then we are condoning a discriminatory system.
>
> (Edwards et al., 2010, p. 12)

Students who, therefore, complete unpaid internships and pay tuition to complete an internship course are, in effect, paying twice as much for an internship experience. When that happens in summer, when tuition is higher, those costs multiply. Are we as an institution, then, creating and perpetuating financial barriers that breed structural discrimination? A case in point from California State University, Long Beach in the summer 2023: A cross-college internship course was cancelled due to low enrollment (total four). While two students were able to substitute the internship class, the others—one, an international student and the other, studying abroad—sought alternatives, such as taking the course in the fall, which defeats the purpose of enrolling in a concurrent internship class and sacrifices quality and student safety. In a related vein, the cancellation itself—fiscal responsibility aside—recalls the question of value. Despite one-on-one outreach, students were not clamoring for the opportunity, even paid ones. Anecdotally, excuses ranged from summer tuition fees to perceived irrelevancy. This is an indication that universities need to better articulate the merit of a concurrent internship course, regardless of degree objectives. Additionally, it is time to consider alternatives, such as free or discounted summer internship courses (given that for many, summer is the only time to schedule an internship), donor-backed initiatives, and other potential financial support structures.

Smaller-scale solutions, such as establishing an endowment, relying on donors, and partnering with public entities to reinforce the idea of a "communiversity," represent other creative—albeit less-than-stable—ways to fund internships, particularly shorter term or summer ones. Smith College's Praxis Program, founded in 1998, provides approximately 400 students per year with $2,000 for summer internships which, according to their website, include "health care, government, education, communications, research, social welfare, technology, law, science and the arts" (Smith College, n.d., para. 1). Smith is forthcoming in recognizing that "many students cannot afford to forgo earnings," which this program addresses (Smith College, n.d., para. 2). Connecticut College (The College Internship Program), Harvard University (Director's Internship Program), and Amherst College (Charles Hamilton Houston Internship Program) (2023) have similar, salaried summer programs with specific eligibility criteria.

Additionally, Gray (2021) spotlights the Sarasota-Manatee Arts & Humanities (SMAH) Internship Program at New College of Florida (2023) that targets the Liberal Arts. Developed and launched during Spring 2020 to fund the first cycle of internships during Fall 2021, the SMAH Internship Program is community driven. Local employers submit internship project proposals to the Center for Career Engagement & Opportunity (CEO), which are then reviewed and selected by a committee made up of CEO staff and faculty members from the Division of Humanities. Dwayne Peterson, executive director of career education in the CEO, explains in his interview with Gray why this program is a game-changer: "We know that unpaid internships disproportionately affect female students, students of color, and first-generation students . . . This disproportionality is perpetuated in the arts and humanities" (Gray, 2021, para. 3). An experiential learning requirement currently applies to all students at Florida State University (Farnum-Patronis, 2019). An internship and its corresponding online course are free (of credit and cost) to matriculated students; as a stand-alone, students pay for one unit. The course is taught and managed by a career counselor from FSU Career Center, and a reported 500 students participated in the summer 2021 (Farnum-Patronis, 2019). This model represents a creative, budget-friendly way to offer internships. Still, no pioneering endeavor is without critics, and, as such, we question zero credit for coursework, HIP fidelity, and course integrity (i.e., degrees of peer-interaction, self-reflection, problem-solving, etc.).

While the proliferation of compensated summer internships is a move in the right direction, we nevertheless wonder—in the spirit of provocative praxis—about their semester or yearlong counterparts. Clemson University's On-Campus Internship program, a symbiotic collaboration between the hiring department and the University at large, provides 1,000 students a year with paid, on-campus internships (Clemson University, 2023). This, along with the program at Idaho State University referenced in Chapter 2, are just two examples of lengthier opportunities. Until universities are unable to invest boldly and broadly, this sampling demonstrates how leveraging resources and partnerships can make paid on-campus internship accessible internally.

Could a model that was popular in the mid-twentieth century—the apprenticeship—provide yet another solution to the unpaid internship quandary? Perlin (2011), for one, encourages us to reconsider apprenticeships, the predecessors of modern-day internships (p. 98). In their promising, four-part edited volume, Cerdin and Peretti (2020) make a compelling case from an international perspective. They explain,

> The pedagogical approach is based on several components. It articulates specific and regular theoretical teachings that allow the apprentice to understand the environment in which he will evolve, the rules of the art that he will have to apply and those of the teachings in professional situations, allowing him to familiarize himself, with the help and supervision of an apprenticeship manager, with the complexity of the practice. Work-linked training thus constitutes the keystone of the knowledge-assimilation process.
>
> (p. 4)

Apprenticeships' appeal comes from the multi-directional learning that should qualify any high-impact endeavor. Further, apprenticeships pick up where internships leave off, as they include what companies prize: "not only a transfer of knowledge, but also a long-term experience that is not possible to acquire through a succession of internships of variable duration in different worlds and on heterogeneous themes" (Cerdin & Peretti, 2020, p. 4). Jean Arthius (2020), who penned the preface (Cerdin & Peretti, 2020), shares that financing of apprenticeships can be sustained by an apprenticeship payroll tax, which is based on a French model (p. xvi). Unfortunately, apprenticeships are broadly misunderstood (and in other cases, have union implications), and Cerdin and Peretti (2020) suggest that a rebranding of the term is (rightfully) in order to change public perception: "the word 'apprenticeship' still conveys an image that is not very rewarding, as the collective unconscious equates it with failure, poverty and lack of intelligence" (p. 9), when, in fact, these job-training models harmoniously bring together "the pragmatism of companies and the academic rigor of teachers" (Arthius, 2020, p. xx).

Until the practice of unpaid internships in our EDIA-oriented world comes to a grinding halt, the debate will continue to harbor invisible—and often overlooked—but crucial data. Indeed, those Students of Color who forgo internship opportunities nevertheless figure as indiscernible statistics. They must also be accounted for because, in a nod to provocative praxis, we should ask ourselves why (and take ameliorative measures). We suspect that the more practical answers point to structural hurdles as well as human circumstance, like concurrent, full-time employment; childcare issues; and high-unit majors. We also suspect the answers involve lower university capital reserves (e.g., students not knowing about internships or how to start the process and not being encouraged or enabled to take on one). Together, they inform the notion of intersequity. This matters because internships are often linked to social mobility: "*Not* having access to an internship can be the kiss of death if you want to move up in the world" (Perlin, 2011, p. 165). As a result, amassing data on who does not sign up for internships is just as important as reporting on who does and ultimately provides a more complete picture of equitable practices.

Support to carry out this work can be done creatively with support from leadership, from earmarking funds to compensate groups of students to seeking grant opportunities to leveraging donor and community leaders who themselves might have been, have hosted, or simply champion interns. Engaging both the symbolic and structural frame concepts underscores the power of compelling storytelling and enhances contributive opportunities, respectively. Considering that the conservative estimate of internships in the United States ranges from 1 to 2 million internships annually, a reconceptualization of unpaid internships is in order, if not long overdue (Perlin, 2011, p. 27).

On a positive note, LBCIP and CollegeCorps@the Beach have bucked the trend of unsalaried positions by taking note and ensuring internship compensation to participating students, enabling them to not only take on meaningful, career-impacting internship work but also to hone leadership skills and in some cases, keep their current jobs (College Corps@the Beach, n.d.; Long Beach Community Internship Program, n.d.). College Corps@the Beach, which the

PIs have designed as a two-semester, paid internship opportunity for qualifying students, including those who have AB 540 status, dovetails with some of the most pressing California issues: climate action and environmental justice, food insecurity, and K-12 education with an emphasis on climate literacy. The goal is to create debt-free pathways in college while serving the Long Beach community. While 45 campuses are part of this statewide initiative, only California State University, Long Beach has decided to focus specifically on paid internships (as opposed to service-learning, for example) (College Corps@the Beach, n.d.). While internships only represent 10% of the statewide College Corps initiative, we are encouraged to see other campuses recognizing the need for paid opportunities and hope that the forthcoming data will inspire others to join the movement.

In sum, this chapter at once benefits from and is complicated by the interconnectedness of the topics therein. From advocacy to pedagogy to compensation, it exemplifies if not gives new meaning to the adjective "student-centered." While metrics are vital and often drive internship discussions, this chapter is a testament to the power of the qualitative and humanistic contours that characterize all high-impact practices.

References

Amherst College. (2023). *Charles Hamilton Houston internship program.* https://careers.amherst.edu/channels/houston-program/

Arthius, J. (2020, January 14). Learning by doing. In J. L. Cerdin & J. M. Peretti (Eds.), *Success of apprenticeships: Views of stakeholders on training and learning* (pp. 19–21). Wiley. https://doi.org//10.1002/9781119694793

Baker, V. L., & Griffin, K. A. (2010). Beyond mentoring and advising: Toward understanding the role of faculty "developers" in student success. *About Campus, 14*(6), 2–8. https://doi.org/10.1002/abc.20002

Benedict, B. J., & Rust, M. M. (2016). *IUPUI taxonomy for internship courses.* https://hdl.handle.net/1805/21506

Black Lives Matter. (n.d.). *About: Black Lives Matter.* https://blacklivesmatter.com/about/

Bolman, L. G., & Gallos, J. V. (2011). *Reframing academic leadership.* Jossey-Bass.

Bowman, C. G., & Lipp, M. (2000, April 1). Legal limbo of the student intern: The responsibility of colleges and universities to protect student interns against sexual harassment. *Harvard Women's Law Journal, 23*(Spring), 95–13. https://papers.ssrn.com/sol3/papers.cfm?abstract_id=2125886

Cerdin, J. L., & Peretti, J.-M. (Eds.). (2020). *The success of apprenticeships: Views of stakeholders on training and learning.* John Wiley & Sons. https://doi.org/10.1002/9781119694793

Ciofalo, A. (1988). Legitimacy of internships for academic credit remains controversial. *The Journalism Educator, 43*(4), 25–31. https://doi.org/10.1177/107769588804300404

Clemson University. (2023). *Center for Career and Professional Development.* UPIC: Internships—Clemson Center for Career and Professional Development.

College Corps@the Beach. (n.d.). www.csulb.edu/college-corps
Collins, M. (2020, November). Open the door: Disparities in paid internships. *NACE Journal*. naceweb.org
Connecticut College (n.d.). *Recent internships*. Connecticut College. conncoll.edu
Crenshaw, K. (1989). Demarginalizing the intersection of race and sex: A Black feminist critique of antidiscrimination doctrine, feminist theory and antiracist politics. *University of Chicago Legal Forum*, *8*, 139–167. http://chicagounbound.uchicago.edu/uclf/vol1989/iss1/8
Doyle, A. (2022). Internship opportunities for students of color. *The Balance*. thebalancemoney.com
Drew, K. (2020). *This is what I know about art*. Penguin Random House.
Durack, K. T. (2013, December). Sweating employment: Ethical and legal issues with unpaid student internships. *College Composition and Communication*, *65*(2), 245–272. www.jstor.org/stable/24633840
Edwards, K. A., Hertel-Fernandez, A., & Cauthen, N. K. (2010). *Paving the way through paid internships: A proposal to expand educational and economic opportunities for low-income college students*. Dēmos. PavingWay_PaidInternships_Demos.pdf
Farnum-Patronis, A. (2019, June 13). *Florida State becomes largest university to add experiential learning requirement*. Florida State University News. fsu.edu
Finley, A., McNair, T., & Clayton-Pedersen, A. (2023). Designing equity-centered high-impact practices. In J. Zilvinskis, J. Kinzie, J. Daday, K. O'Donnell, & C. Vande Zande (Eds.), *Delivering on the promise of high-impact practices: Research and models for student success* (pp. 17–29). Stylus Publishing.
Freedland Fisher, J. (2022, May 23). Don't just pay interns, help them build networks. *Harvard Business Review*. hbr.org
Gardener, P. (2011). The debate over unpaid college internships. *Intern Bridge*. psu.edu
Gray, K. (2021, May 17). Funding program for unpaid internships in Arts and Humanities has unique twist. *NACE*. naceweb.org
Harvard University. (2023). *Director's internship program*. The Institute of Politics at Harvard University.
Hora, M. T. (2022a). Internships for all: How inequitable access to internships hinders the promise and potential of high-impact practices and work-based learning. In J. Zilvinskis, J. Kinzie, J. Daday, & K. O'Donnell, & C. Vande Zande (Eds.), *Delivering on the promise of high-impact practices: Research and models for student success* (pp. 113–123). Stylus Publishing.
Hora, M. T. (2022b). *Unpaid internships & inequality: A review of the data and recommendations for research, policy and practice* [Policy brief]. Center for Research on College Workforce Transitions; University of Wisconsin, Madison. https://ccwt.wisc.edu/publication/unpaid-internships-and-inequality-a-review-of-the-data-and-recommendations-for-research-policy-and-practice-policy-brief-2/
Hora, M. T., Chen, Z., Parrott, E., & Her, P. (2020). Problematizing college internships: Exploring issues with access, program design, and developmental outcomes. *International Journal of Work-Integrated Learning*, *21*(3), 235–252.
Hora, M. T., Huerta, A., Gopal, A., & Wolfgram, M. (2021, May). *A review of the literature on internships for Latinx students at Hispanic-serving institutions: Toward a Latinx-serving internship experience* (WCER Working Paper No. 2021-2). University of Wisconsin–Madison, Wisconsin Center for Education Research. WCER_Working_Paper_No_2021-2.pdf (wisc.edu)

Hora, M. T., Wolfgram, M., & Chen, Z. (2019). *Closing the doors of opportunity: How financial, sociocultural and institutional barriers intersect to inhibit participation in college internships* (WCER Working Paper No. 2019-8). University of Wisconsin–Madison, Wisconsin Center for Education Research. Microsoft Word-Barriers kf2Paper_WCERWP_120219_ZC.docx (wisc.edu)

Insight into Diversity. (2021). Unpaid internships continue to be a prominent—yet inequitable—career pathway. *Insight into Diversity*. https://www.insightintodiversity.com/unpaid-internships-continue-to-be-a-prominent-yet-inequitable-career-pathway/#:~:text=Unpaid%20Internships%20Continue%20to%20be%20a%20Prominent%20%E2%80%94%20Yet%20Inequitable%20%E2%80%94%20Career%20Pathway,-By%20INSIGHT%20Staff&text=A%20new%20survey%20report%20from,often%20come%20with%20these%20experiences.

Kinzie, J., McCormick, A. C., Gonyea, R. M., Dugan, B., & Silberstein, S. (2021). Getting beyond the label: Three takes on quality in high-impact practices. *Liberal Education.* aacu.org

Kinzie, J., Silberstein, S., McCormick, A. C., Gonyea, R. M., & Dugan, B. (2021). Centering racially minoritized student voices in high-impact practices. *Change, 53*(4), 6–14. https://doi.org/10.1080/00091383.2021.1930976

Kuh, G. D. (2008). High-impact educational practices: What they are, who has access to them, and why they matter. *Peer Review, 14*(3), 29.

Lo, T. (2011). *Realities: A collection of short stories.* CreateSpace Independent Publishing Platform.

Long Beach Community Internship Program. (n.d.). *Mission and goals.* California State University Long Beach. csulb.edu

McNair, T. B., Bensimon, E. M., & Malcom-Piqueux, L. (2020). *From equity talk to equity walk: Expanding practitioner knowledge for racial justice in higher education.* Jossey-Bass. https://doi.org/10.1002/9781119428725

Moncada, M. S. (2017). The whole is greater: My turn to tell the story: Internships for people of color. *History News, 72*(1), 5–6.

National Association of Colleges and Employers. (n.d.-b). *Unpaid internships and the need for federal action.* Position statement: U.S. internships. naceweb.org

New College of Florida. (2023). *Career prep program.* www.ncf.edu/ceo/

Norman, J. (2021, March 31). *Internship for credit: Gaining experience or getting scammed?* The Berkeley Beacon.

O'Neill, N. (2010). Internships as a high-impact practice: Some reflections on quality. *Peer Review, 12*(4), 4–8.

Perlin, R. (2011). *Intern nation: How to earn nothing and learn little in the brave new economy.* Verso.

Reeves, R. V. (2017). *Dream hoarders: How the American upper middle class is leaving everyone else in the dust, why that is a problem, and what to do.* Brookings Institution Press.

Rojas, L., Stormes, K., Manke, B., & Ocular. G. (2021, May 14). *Assessing internships: For whom and under what circumstances are academic internships a high-impact practice?* [Poster presentation]. CSULB Data Fellows Annual Symposium, Long Beach, CA.

Rothschild, P. C., & Rothschild, C. L. (2020). The unpaid internship: Benefits, drawbacks, and legal issues. *Administrative Issues Journal: Connecting Education, Practice, and Research, 10*(2), 1–17. https://doi.org/10.5929/2020.10.2.1

Smith College. (n.d.). *Praxis program*. Smith College.

Steinmetz, K. (2020). She coined the term 'intersectionality' over 30 years ago. Here's what it means to her today. *Time*. https://time.com/5786710/kimberle-crenshaw-intersectionality/

Thijssen, F. S. L., & Kessel, S. (2021, December 13). Nepotism and networks: Inequity in internship access for students. *The Tufts Daily*. https://www.tuftsdaily.com/article/2021/12/nepotism-and-networks-inequity-in-internship-access-for-students

Verschelden, C. (2017). *Bandwidth recovery: Helping students reclaim cognitive resources lost to poverty, racism, and social marginalization*. Stylus Publishing.

Waddoups, G. L., Wentworth, N., & Rodney, E. (2004). Principles of technology integration and curriculum development. *Computers in the Schools*, *21*(1–2), 15–23. https://doi.org/10.1300/J025v21n01_02

Yosso, T. J. (2005). Whose culture has capital? A critical race theory discussion of community cultural wealth. *Race, Ethnicity and Education*, *8*(1), 69–91. https://doi.org/10.1080/1361332052000341006

4 Community Partners as Critical Coefficients in the Internship Equation

When talking about equitable internship experiences, who has a seat at the table matters. All too often, community partners, the people, and organizations that host our student interns, are not included, or considered, in important conversations about internship programming. In fact, host agencies are often taken for granted, or even excluded, in the internship-as-a-system discussion. Provocative praxis in this chapter includes asking particularly tough questions about why we often fail to develop authentic partnerships with the community organizations that host our student interns, how to train site supervisors who provide critical mentoring and support to interns, with a focus on investigating the role of intersectionality and the mentoring relationship, and the role (if any) that community partners can play in shaping university internship curriculum. Several leadership frameworks come into play in these discussions as building partnerships and providing training involve marshaling human resources, constructing policies and procedures, framing initiatives in ways that promote buy-in, and leveraging our allies (Bolman & Gallos, 2011). Instead of highlighting one case study, we take a different approach in this chapter and highlight several case studies to illustrate the many ways we might cultivate and maintain partnerships with sites that host our student interns.

Cultivating authentic partnerships with community organizations

Authentic internship partnerships begin with those vested in their success. Students, university internship coordinators, internship-course-teaching faculty, and community partners must understand and cultivate their interrelationships for the internship to be successful. Each participant has a unique role in the relationship to ensure quality internship experiences that are truly for the benefit of the student (see "benefit burden" in Chapter 1). How, then, do we authentically engage with businesses, agencies, and community partners to create meaningful and impactful partnerships and opportunities for our students? What do authentic partnerships look like in practical terms, and what are common challenges in developing authentic partnerships?

DOI: 10.4324/9781003296324-4

One answer might be that we (erroneously) believe that we hold all the expertise and that the flow of knowledge is unidirectional if not unilateral. This seems ironically counterintuitive to the core values of higher education, including curiosity, lifelong learning, and collaboration. Why, then, are some faculty resistant to engaging in conversations around internships or career development? As discussed in Chapter 2, the answers include some might not be willing to give up control and open the door for constructive feedback and collaboration from industry, while others argue that the university is not a vocational school and career readiness is not their expertise or job. These refusals can lead faculty to disengage from the conversation altogether, and ultimately limit opportunities for students to learn, become aware of internship opportunities, and connect with, industry professionals. This hypothesis is exemplified in a July 2022 report from California Competes, which indicates that:

> Faculty, particularly those outside the occupational and professional fields, seem to have little engagement with employers. Interviewees mentioned the challenge of shifting faculty mindsets to see employers as meaningful contributors to students' postsecondary experiences, particularly with regard to the content of programs and courses.
>
> (p. 4)

Furthermore, the California Competes (2022) report identified three distinct barriers institutions of higher education and employers face when trying to build partnerships. These barriers include a disconnect in organizational culture, difficulties navigating bureaucracy, and values misalignment:

> Both industry and higher education representatives noted ways that differences between their respective organizational cultures hinder responsive, timely, and ongoing collaboration to support a pathway for students to enter the workforce. The cultural differences often fostered discord in the development of structures, communications, motivations, and perspectives.
>
> (p. 4)

An example of a bureaucratic misalignment that limits our ability to engage authentically includes navigating contexts where the cycles of work are different. Colleges work on a quarter or semester calendar and structure their internship classes to align with academic calendars. However, most people outside of the college context do not schedule their work around academic calendars. When universities structure their internship programs along quarter or semester timelines, it is not always compatible with recruitment cycles and needs. How can we be more flexible to the realities of the industry instead of demanding partners to align with academic calendars? For example, can internship classes have flexible start dates and offer variable unit options to meet the needs of students and organizations. How does creating a more flexible structure impact accurate tracking of internships and faculty workload? Forming authentic relationships is complicated when higher education and industry understand "career readiness" differently. In a 2020 study conducted by the Association of Public and Land-grant Universities, Crawford and Fink (2020) found that there was a discrepancy between career readiness expectations of employers and faculty. Each stakeholder was asked "to rate how important a skill was, rate how prepared students were in that skill, and to rank what activities outside the classroom most contributed to learning these skills" (p. 2). The largest preparedness gap for employers was the skill "Understanding role and expectations in the workplace" (p. 3). Where employers rated this as the largest skill gap, faculty placed this number 9 of 11.

One of our long-standing internship partners, Micah Giles, Marketing Director of Kids Sports News Network (KSSN), exemplifies this finding (M. Giles, personal communication, March 1, 2023). As the internship coordinator for KSNN for the past 15 years, she has supervised and mentored countless interns. She noted that what most interns lack is having realistic expectations and knowing how to engage with colleagues in the workplace. Some might argue that that is the purpose of the internship, for students to learn those skills, but could we be doing a better job of working with industry partners to prepare our students and set them up for success at their internships? Giles provides examples such as inviting internship partners into the classroom as guest lecturers or collaborating with organizations to implement real-world projects within the classroom. These early exposures to industry and application of theory to practice can help better prepare students and engage all parties in deeper, more meaningful partnerships that ultimately benefit students. Giles also encourages annual or bi-annual meetings with partnering organizations to share feedback with faculty and staff and vice versa, enabling industry partners to network with university faculty and staff through the mutual sharing of best practices (M. Giles, personal communication, March 1, 2023). Activities like these show organizations that the university is truly vested in developing authentic, symbiotic partnerships. If community and employer partners are ready to collaborate to engage with us, let's find meaningful ways to meet them halfway.

On a larger scale, campus bureaucracy and structure also cause challenges for employers to navigate policies, paperwork, and risk management requirements, especially if these vary across campuses. From the California Competes report, "Interviewees mentioned most the need for both employers and higher education institutions to build and support internal and external structures to help institutionalize their partnerships" (p. 6). This is further complicated and frustrating when employers need to figure out different requirements from different departments on the same campus, which makes partnering across the university a challenge. As referenced in Chapter 2, a coordinated entry point into campuses for organizations to inquire about hosting internships can be a way to simplify the process for employers. This gateway can help eliminate the confusion for employers and level the playing field for smaller community organizations to connect with the university. It does not require that the organization have a dedicated recruitment team or a personal relationship with someone from the university, but that instead, it makes the connection process transparent for any organization that is interested in hosting a student intern. As we ponder internship equity for students, we also need to consider our partners and structure equitable practices with our community partners. By having a systemized entry point for employers and community agencies, we simplify the process and, by making access easier for partners, expand diverse opportunities for students.

As we discuss how to develop authentic partnerships, we also must consider the geographical context in which the institutions and organizations operate. In rural areas or small communities, host sites may be limited, either in terms of a number of opportunities or to local industries. This can be particularly problematic when internships are curricular requirements. Institutions cited in Lopes et al.'s (2019) study provide two specific strategies for enhancing and protecting current internship offerings. First, they advertised the "supply side of interns" in local newspapers to increase internship placements. Then, to strengthen existing partnerships, they established an advisory committee, which includes members who host student interns, so that partners felt they had a voice in the process (Lopes et al., 2019). In tandem, they forged new opportunities while enhancing current partnerships. To remedy other geographical challenges, virtual internships represent another viable solution, with the caveat that virtual internships are not always the best option for students. While a remote internship offers flexibility, it comes at a cost. Students who need more structure, guidance, and mentorship might struggle or fail in a virtual setting. Unless the organization is intentional in engaging the intern, the student risks forfeiting a significant benefit of an internship, networking opportunities, and making professional connections.

During the COVID-19 pandemic, organizations had to pivot without sacrificing quality and intentionality in online modalities. The National Association of Colleges and Employers (NACE) showcased a successful virtual internship from a small New England non-profit, Commonwealth Care Alliance who has a one-person university relation and recruiting (URR) office (Gray, 2021). With the help of an internship committee, comprised of employees in the human resources department, Jesse Shearer, the sole URR employee, collaborates with the HR department to coordinate onboarding, orientations, trainings, and networking events. The number of interns they take on each summer depends on the capacity of the mentors, to provide quality, meaningful experiences, as Shearer explains:

> We budget to hire 15 to 25 interns each summer, however, we want to ensure that we have thoughtful and meaningful projects for the interns to work on, so the number of available projects and departments able to mentor an intern drive the number we will hire.
>
> (para. 7)

Awareness and realistic expectations help ensure a quality internship experience for the students, and this, in turn, improves intern satisfaction rates and increases the intern-to-employee conversion rate.

Organizations often provide opportunities beyond the internship description. Cynthia Hernandez (C. Hernandez, personal communication, February 10, 2023), the Program Director for Los Angeles-based Well-Suited, a nonprofit for underrepresented junior high and high school students, shares how they provide wrap-around support for their student interns, who are not only mentored by the Program Director on their own personal and professional development but who also trained to mentor program participants. From orientation to completion of the internships, student interns engage in their own career exploration and career readiness activities. Well-Suited also invites industry experts, such as marketing and public relations professionals, to present and network with student interns. Upon program completion, interns become members of the Well-Suited Club House, with ongoing access to career advising and professional support. Employers such as Commonwealth Care Alliance and Well-Suited engage industry professionals to create valuable opportunities for students to develop industry knowledge, skills, and help interns design their own career paths. Their holistic rather than linear approach to internships could serve as a new, twenty-first century model.

The Commonwealth Care Alliance and Well-Suited virtual internship programs boast internal infrastructure to support high-impact internships, but not all organizations are "intern ready." The ways universities reach and vet potential partners are often haphazard at best. Especially with unpaid internships, it is imperative that the internship incorporates the Four I's referenced in Chapter 1: intensity, intention, interaction, and integration. The challenges associated with identifying if an organization is an appropriate internship site depend greatly upon their status as "intern ready" (i.e., assuring adequate internship placements where students are primary beneficiaries of benefits and are not exploited as free labor). Recently, a potential California State University, Long Beach partnering agency confessed that they needed an intern as a stopgap measure. Comments such as these should be a red flag to universities placing students, as interns should not be viewed in this way (i.e., as replacements for salaried employees). Even well-meaning organizations encounter issues when they fail to differentiate between volunteers and interns, to provide enough professional work for an intern, or to train and house dedicated mentors and supervisors. Sometimes good intentions fall short, and it is important that universities and organizations engage in honest and open conversations about the expectations (and demands) of hosting a student intern. The student will only be enabled for a quality experience if the organization is ready to take on the responsibility of ensuring it.

Having those honest conversations with internship partners can be difficult and uncomfortable. On the university side, severing a relationship before it even begins is never optimal, so finding ways to achieve internship readiness is a matter of good communication. These conversations can help mitigate larger problems down the line. Otherwise, the lack of intervention creates chaos, as exemplified in one department at California State University, Long Beach that had multiple students interning at a local daycare center. As the semester began, students shared some of their concerns about the internship site, such as not being provided adequate training, being assigned repeated, menial tasks like preparing snacks and cleaning toys, and even being left unsupervised with children. For the safety of the student interns and the children at the daycare, the department immediately removed the student interns from the site, and the site was flagged as predatory for using unpaid student interns to fill staff positions. Another example included a student working in a clinical setting in a privately owned physical therapy office. The student intern was being trained to use medical equipment with patients without appropriate certification. The student voiced their concerns and, once again, the department put a moratorium on the internship. We wonder, then, how pervasive this is in the internship world. Having a scaffolded internship system, which we reference throughout this book, helps minimize these dangerous situations and vacuous experiences.

Furthermore, universities can take a proactive approach in this process when vetting new opportunities and partnerships. For example, the College Corps program at California State University, Long Beach hosts mandatory orientations for participating organizations. The orientation covers best practices for mentoring, providing feedback, and training student interns. College Corps intentionally invites anyone who will be supervising a student intern, not just executive directors, to the orientation. It is important that the person who will be working directly with the student intern is present and understands (and is willing to take on) their role as internship site supervisor. We discuss training site supervisors in more detail later in this chapter.

Cultivating authentic partnerships, therefore, takes vulnerability, namely the willingness to accept that no one party, university, or host site has all the answers; we must welcome the idea of multi-directional learning. As Micah Giles from KSNN asserts, the most valuable characteristic of forming authentic partnerships is:

> Both parties being able to look at the student needs, see from each other's perspective, and understand who is going to provide what kind of support to the student. We need to be better at understanding where each parties' strengths lie and be willing to go beyond our comfort zone to work truly collectively.
>
> (M. Giles, personal communication, March 1, 2023)

Universities and internship partners need to engage in earnest conversations about the workload of coordinating internship programs to ensure quality experiences for student interns. This is what ultimately brings value to the partnering organization. As Lopes et al. (2019) suggest, universities could strengthen existing, exemplary partnerships through the establishment of an advisory committee with local businesses and organizations. Frequent and transparent conversations about challenges and successes from both sides can ameliorate relationships and experiences for all. Furthermore, universities and organizations should assess their own infrastructures to bolster recruitment pipelines and institutionalize partnerships so that they do not just exist with a single faculty or staff member or within a single department. As discussed in Chapter 2, having a central point of contact for internship partners and adequately staffing or implementing a centralized staffing approach to support growing internship initiatives can address this challenge. While there is no one-size-fits-all solution, there is a need to acknowledge and respond to the local context, factors, and forces that impact our ability to engage in authentic partnerships.

Partners as supervisors who provide support and mentoring

Despite the common belief that interns' tasks lie at the heart of an internship, in fact students' interactions with their supervisors are what yield transformative internship experiences. As a result, an agency's perceived status as a mere practical, passive component thus warrants reconsideration. Agencies are not simply receptacles into which students are deposited to gain real-world experience. As McHugh (2017) asserts:

> Interns require a more intensive integration effort than typical organisational newcomers because interns are seeking both narrow (skill development) and broad (career development) learning experiences in a condensed time frame, as well as care because of their likely fragile sense of workplace self.
>
> (p. 370)

As such, site supervisors' responsibilities can include not only task assignments but also ongoing support and mentoring. Support comes in many forms, but ultimately signals to interns that a supervisor genuinely cares about their well-being and workplace contributions. Affirming an intern's value as a person, paying attention to psychological and emotional wellbeing, expressing appreciation, and demonstrating respect all constitute support. In contrast, mentoring, while certainly another manifestation of support, focuses more on providing interns with clear direction and feedback on task performance, guidance to find solutions to challenges, hone specific strategies for achieving career goals, cultivate networking opportunities, and introduce interns to the culture of work and the specific norms of the profession (Hora et al., 2020).

As Kupersmidt et al. (2019) confirm, mentors are the unsung heroes of the internship equation:

> We have strong evidence that mentors can help young people build their identities as workers, help them apply their school learning to work, teach them soft skills that can be essential to career success, improve their attitudes and motivations about work, and generally give young workers opportunities to learn new skills and how to be part of a team. This sets the stage for ongoing career success and tangible rewards, such as higher compensation, advancement up career ladders, and greater job stability.
>
> (p. 7)

As a result, supervisor support and mentoring strongly and positively correlate with various internship outcomes. Supervisor support facilitates learning as interns are more likely to ask questions and explore their strengths and weaknesses when there is a safe space to do so (McHugh, 2017). Both supervisor support and mentoring are related to internship satisfaction (D'Abate et al., 2009; Hora, Chen, et al., 2020) and organizational attraction—an intern's intent to pursue a job with the hosting organization after their internship is completed (McHugh, 2017). The benefits of consistent supervisor support and mentoring may be particularly important for students completing e-internships (i.e., remote or virtual placements): "Having mentors benefits organisations by reducing silent drop-out, which is important as dropping out of an e-internship is significantly easier than leaving a traditional internship" (Jeske & Linehan, 2020, p. 253). That is, students in virtual internship placements who are struggling to stay engaged are more likely to persist if they have support and mentoring from a supervisor.

In short, supervisors are key to making interns feel like they matter and providing opportunities for interns to learn and thrive. Thus, when agencies match interns with a supervisor, the process should involve staff who possess established mentoring skills as well as a reputation for being supportive. Supervisors' importance cannot be overstated, as these individuals often become catalysts for exemplifying achievement, while providing concrete examples of behaviors and approaches that lead to success. Supervisors represent to interns not only what the agency stands for—namely, their mission and culture—but also what the entire profession has to offer and how the intern fits (or not): "By identifying with an outstanding role model, individuals can become inspired to pursue similar achievements" (Lockwood, 2006, p. 36). In our own work, we have heard interns say anecdotally that supervisors who provided excellent mentoring inspired them to follow in their supervisors' footsteps (i.e., to model such behavior in their own mentoring opportunities). In contrast, we have likewise (and lamentably) learned that unsupportive supervisors prompted some interns to rethink pursuing careers in their chosen fields of interest altogether.

Although research studies are quick to acknowledge the significance of supervisor support and mentoring, rarely discussed are the challenges to balancing these roles successfully. Being a mentor and supervisor can be time consuming and contradictory. It may be hard, for example, to provide support while simultaneously providing direct feedback about an intern's performance, especially when corrective action must be taken. In cases where direct supervisors do not provide both support and mentoring, organizations may want to assign another person within the organization to serve as an intern's mentor (D'Abate et al., 2009). This distributive supervisory approach—whereby an intern is mentored and supported by multiple people in the organization— "can offer mentees broader perspectives and can alleviate negative mentoring experiences where there is conflict with a primary mentoring figure" (Kupersmidt et al., 2019, p. 10). When shared mentoring is not possible and conflicts arise between supervisors and interns, mentor training focused on managing difficult relationships may be necessary if supervisors are to reconcile being an intern's cheerleader and their coach.

Conversely, making multiple employees responsible for a student's internship experience can generate other challenges. McHugh (2017) asks, "Can an organization that lacks the financial resources to compensate interns, at the same time, devote sufficient resources to provide a high-level of supervisor mentoring and support that are apparently so vital to a successful internship experience?" (p. 379). To provide effective mentoring and support, organizations need a robust mentoring culture where there is buy-in across the agency for supervising efforts. Not unlike providing infrastructural support for internship programming on university campuses (see Chapter 2), this need for buy-in evokes the human resource, structural, and symbolic leadership frames (Bolman & Gallos, 2011). In essence, to effectively host interns, organizations need people (employees) willing to supervise interns, company policies that explicitly state that supervising interns is legitimate work, and a culture that recognizes supervisory work as worthy of public recognition/reward, tied to the mission and vision of the company. With company backing and site supervisor commitment to providing effective mentoring and support, student interns have the best chance for success, of experiencing their internships as beneficial and transformative.

Training site supervisors

Because formal training of site supervisors is not yet ubiquitous, the quality of intern supervision varies considerably from site to site. As Hora, Wolfgram, et al. (2020) note in their study using both surveys and focus groups, some site supervisors take an active approach to coaching their student interns, whereas others provide little support or feedback on task performance. If we subscribe to the belief that all site supervisors are interested in providing quality internship experiences for students (currently, a debatable proposition), we are obligated to provide training to internship supervisors, who do not necessarily have experience in delegating, providing feedback, or leading with empathy. In fact, many lack all three, and working with interns may be, in fact, their first foray into supervising others, which is unfair to both novice supervisors and student interns.

This then begs the question: *who* should be trained? Is training mandatory for all tentative supervisors, or do tangential experiences, including prior mentoring experience, qualify one as a competent site host supervisor and mentor? In their examination of mentors who worked with entrepreneurs, St.-Jean and Mitrano-Meda (2016) found that prior mentoring experience may not be a good indicator that a person has the capacity to be a suitable mentor. Specifically, having prior mentoring experience did not necessarily enhance the relationship between mentor and mentee nor was it related to greater learning on the part of the mentee—in fact, it was the opposite:

> Mentor training is only marginally useful for new mentors, but is crucial for experienced mentors and can help neutralize the negative effect of accumulated experience. It would, therefore, appear that training allows mentors to question their intervention and help them maintain an awareness of the psychosocial aspects of mentoring.
>
> (p. 52)

Similarly, Gandhi and Johnson (2016) report that without ongoing training, supervisors may mimic mentors they have had in the past, with mixed results. We thus argue that site supervisor training is important for everyone, that it warrants a dedicated training, and that it should be ongoing rather than a one-time event. We recognize, however, that requiring all site supervisors to attend some sort of training, even if it is only a basic orientation where new host sites are onboarded and provided information about university expectations, takes time (on the part of both supervisors and university staff) and involves resources.

Once it is determined who should be trained to supervise interns, we must also consider what content to include in these trainings, including what can reasonably be taught. Undoubtedly there are characteristics or dispositions of good supervisors that may be difficult or even impossible to teach. In Cho et al.'s (2011) analysis of letters of recommendation for mentoring awards, several ideal mentoring characteristics emerged including personal qualities: kindness, honesty, generosity, and selflessness. But are these qualities learnable? As a possible work-around, we might think about ways to select supervisors who already possess these characteristics and, focus instead on program requirements, mentoring best practices, and cultural competency that dovetail with "evidence-informed training materials with content that combines findings from research literature, input from practitioners, and feedback from trainees to create training practices that are well-grounded in the literature and best practices of the field" (Garringer et al., 2015, p. 47).

Coverage of program requirements is likely the most straightforward component of training, as it focuses on what the university expects of site supervisors including practical matters such as tracking hours, providing feedback on interns' performance, and adhering to university policies on safety, confidentiality of student information, liability, and non-discrimination. It is also important to clarify the differences between interns, volunteers, and employees so that supervisors can establish reasonable expectations of their student interns. From there, supervisors are better positioned to implement appropriate boundaries and work with interns to set learning goals.

Establishing realistic expectations also involves the preparation of students. Some students have unrealistic expectations for what their relationships with their supervisors will be like. Others may be unaware of the importance of demonstrating initiative and drive, being receptive to feedback and coaching, actively seeking opportunities to learn, and being open to collaboration. Knowing what to expect helps all parties be prepared. Discussions between students, supervisors, and university representatives about expectations can also impact satisfaction such that the greater the match between internship expectations and students' actual experiences, the greater students' overall satisfaction with their internship experiences (Neelam et al., 2019).

Training content focused on best practices for mentoring typically emphasizes relationship-enhancing behaviors like frequent and regular contact with interns (Cho et al., 2011; Spiekermann et al., 2021), clear communication of tasks to be completed (Bhattacharya & Neelam, 2018), and reflective listening (Kupersmidt et al., 2019). Other training topics focused on the interactions between mentors and interns include the provision of regular performance feedback (Bhattacharya & Neelam, 2018), and the willingness of mentors to acknowledge a mentees' personal life and potential challenges to meeting internship expectations (Cho et al., 2011; Hora, Chen, et al., 2020). Helping site supervisors that develop relational competence is paramount, especially for those who never acquired these skills in their own professional journeys.

Less frequently covered, but equally important, is training supervisors to identify appropriately challenging tasks for interns, develop learning goals with students, scaffold learning, and create opportunities where students can realize their potential. Previous studies suggest that task autonomy—flexibility on how work is completed and discretion on task assignments—is a particularly onerous component of intern supervision to master, as it involves both well-crafted tasks and recognizing an intern's thresholds (Hora, Wolfgram, et al., 2020). Autonomy has a direct correlation to trust, as well as prompt problem solving and decreased passivity, as interns are more likely to take initiative if given the latitude to make decisions. Although this may benefit certain interns, it may prove disastrous for others. Excessive autonomy can be frustrating for an intern who sees self-direction as neglect; too much autonomy can even lead interns down paths that are ultimately unproductive. These interns need guidance and direction and languish unless they have more structured tasks (Lave & Wenger, 1991). This is why it is crucial for supervisors to familiarize themselves with their interns' working style and to proceed accordingly. Supervisor training might be a space in which to shed light on how to balance autonomy with support. Hora, Wolfgram, et al. (2020) suggest a process of co-participation whereby supervisors demonstrate how to complete tasks with interns assisting on the margins. Over time as interns gain confidence and skills, supervisors can step back and allow interns to take the reins. Hora, Wolfgram, et al. (2020) underscore the collaborative yet independent currents of such a process:

> In this way, the supervisor remains central to the activity system, but through work that is scaffolded and facilitated by the supervisor-intern interaction, the intern gradually becomes more central to the activity system, displaying competence and independence, and acquiring an identity of a novice professional.
>
> (p. 25)

Cultural competency and diversity training figure as another area ripe for inclusion in supervisor preparation. Supervisors should be encouraged to interrogate their own cultural biases about background and demographic characteristics (Garringer et al., 2015), while mentors should check in with themselves:

> Mentors must also recognize the privilege that has been afforded to them not just in their position of power in the workplace, but also their potential positions of power with regards to their racial identity, gender identity, and sexual orientation, for example.
>
> (Kupersmidt et al., 2019, p. 64)

Other diversity-adjacent topics that relate to supervisor onboarding might include discrimination, linguistic racism, and microaggressions. Without frank discussions of these topics, a supervisor with relatively more privilege may be unaware of their student interns' site experiences, especially those from historically marginalized racial groups and those who are the first in their families to go to college. Or worse, supervisors could reproduce racial/class/gender inequalities if not intentional about acknowledging students' backgrounds:

> Training that includes issues surrounding race and discrimination can have the added benefit of teaching mentors to deal effectively with their own unconscious biases and can help build their empathy for and advocacy skills on behalf of their mentees . . . Mentors should understand how to help their mentees address these issues in the workplace should they arise. However, the most important thing to include in mentor training is to learn

to avoid compounding any trauma experienced by their mentees, by intervening on their behalf.

(Kupersmidt et al., 2019, p. 65)

Diversity and ally training should go beyond simply "doing no harm" or refraining from making students' past or current experiences of discrimination and trauma worse. Ultimately, we are responsible for preparing site supervisors to recognize and foster the knowledge, skills, and assets that students bring with them to college. Perhaps the key, as Luedke (2017) suggests, is for mentors and role models to create counter spaces—"academic or social spaces where deficit perspectives can be negated and where students' experiences are validated and acknowledged" (p. 50). These safe spaces can provide alternatives to negative images and racial stereotypes and shield students from messaging that suggests the suppression of parts of their identity (McCoy et al., 2015).

Supervisors are called to support students holistically and to not only acknowledge students' multiple identities but also ponder how these identities converge to reinforce privilege or inequities (see "intersequity" in Chapter 3). Supervisors have a duty to adopt approaches—like Yosso's (2005) community cultural wealth model—that value students' diverse backgrounds. The capital that students bring with them to college may be given different values depending on the context in which they are viewed. Internship sites, unfortunately, may be one context where, for example, resistance capital—the experience of challenging inequality and pursuing equal rights—is not valued (Luedke et al., 2023). Likewise, internship sites may not recognize as helpful the wisdom, values, and stories students draw from their extended families and community networks (i.e., familial capital). How might student interns' experiences on-site be different if their skills learned and acquired by maneuvering racially biased systems and confronting inequality as an everyday lived reality were recognized and celebrated by their site supervisors?

Some argue that validating students, acknowledging the cultural capital they bring, and creating counter spaces that honor their authentic selves happen more readily when students are matched with supervisors on similar background characteristics like race, ethnicity, gender, and first-generation college status. In fact, there is growing consensus (e.g., Hora, Chen, et al., 2020; Santos & Reigadas, 2002) that students' demographic backgrounds may affect the supervisory relationship—especially that between Students of Color and white supervisors. People of Color in leadership positions have lived experiences to draw from, which make them the ideal mentors and coaches for Students of Color in these contexts. Where a white person's empathy ends is where a Person of Color can speak directly to how she has addressed racist hiring practices or found her voice when others have tried to erase her contributions. While we recognize that it is always not possible to do this sort of identity matching, making the effort to pair students with mentors that have similar lived experiences makes sense. In a similar way, gender-matching mentors and mentees confer similar benefits, especially for women: "When members of a group are in the minority in a particular occupation, or are stereotyped as being incompetent in that career domain, it may be especially important for them to know that someone like themselves has been successful" (Lockwood, 2006, p. 45). Contrastively, being coupled with a potential role model who has more privilege may be less inspirational.

We wonder: What is the mechanism that drives the benefits of matched mentoring pairs? Do white mentors unintentionally devalue students' prior capital? Are white mentors uncomfortable acknowledging their mentees' racial and ethnic backgrounds and how those backgrounds impact student success? Luedke's (2017) pivotal study of Students of Color and their role models identifies three themes. First, Mentors of Color nurtured the various forms of capital that Students of Color brought with them to college. They

> nurtured prior capital by prioritizing students as whole individuals whose status as students was only a piece of their identity. In these relationships, students could let their guard down and be themselves in a place where they would be appreciated for who they were and the experiences they brought with them to college.
>
> (Luedke, 2017, p. 44)

Second, as authentic relationships developed, Mentors of Color were committed to transparency and honesty. Students received constructive feedback that allowed them to take corrective action, work on skills needing improvement, and brainstorm ways to address challenges. And finally, Mentors of Color made themselves readily available to their mentees. In contrast,

> White staff and administrators focused on students' academic experiences and neglected other factors that affected their role as students such as personal or familial concerns. Because of these interactions, students overwhelmingly felt these individuals did not attempt to build genuine relationships with them.
>
> (Luedke, 2017, p. 43)

McCoy et al. (2015) note that furthermore, some mentors with good intentions profess to be colorblind, understood as the commitment to treating all students the same way, regardless of race or ethnicity:

> While the idea of 'treating students the same' sounds reasonable at first glance, there can be implicit problems to this approach to mentoring . . . a colorblind approach can actually work to erase students' backgrounds, or this could imply that all students should assimilate to a Eurocentric way of thinking, behaving, and speaking.
>
> (p. 233)

The upshot: interns feeling they do not belong. Further, a colorblind approach gives mentors permission to ignore the real and important structural inequities faced by Students of Color.

Despite the findings that matching interns and site supervisors (mentors) on background characteristics may confer benefits to students, we acknowledge that targeted matching may not be feasible on a large scale. Not only would matching be time consuming and complicated (Which background characteristics do you match on when several seem relevant?), we can imagine programs having difficulty identifying enough supervisors at their hosting sites with the same ethnic or racial background characteristics as interns, especially for those internship programs designed specifically for Students of Color. Perhaps there is an alternative to uncritically advocating for matching that circles back to the topic of training. Luedke (2017) suggests that knowing how matched mentors benefit their mentees provides an opportunity to better prepare white mentors to support marginalized student populations in ways that value their backgrounds: "Treating students as persons first, and students second, acknowledges their rich cultural backgrounds and creates an environment where students can share their capital as well as acquire additional forms of capital" (p. 50).

Tu and Li (2021) suggest something similar, although not necessarily in reference to racial or ethnic matching of supervisors. That is, one of the key components of effective mentoring is to build rapport: "mutual trust and respect, shared understanding of one another's values and perspectives, and strong communication" (p. 3). In effect, they encourage holistic mentoring such that mentees are encouraged to talk about their lives outside of work. They note that "investing time in meaningful, deep connections with individuals one-on-one can be a refreshing change and chance for more authentic connection" (p. 4). They highlight that "you cannot talk meaningfully about careers without talking about the source of your motivations, about family, and about life's highs and lows" (p. 5).

Further, Ensher et al. (2002) suggest that we need to probe more deeply for similarity around attitudes (e.g., having similar values about work) and not rely simply on surface-level similarity. Having similar attitudes may be a better predictor than demographic similarities in predicting mentor support and a mentee's satisfaction with their mentors: "Promoting an active awareness regarding the importance of perceived attitudinal similarity and genuine willingness to accept demographic dissimilarity is an important component of successful diverse mentoring relationships" (Ensher et al., 2002, p. 1423).

The final component of site supervisor training deals with delivery and mode of training. We contend that universities bear responsibility for ensuring that site supervisors have adequate training and if necessary, to resource it in the absence of other alternatives. Such training efforts should be tailored to the group of supervisors and their interns as one size does not fit all (St.-Jean & Mitrano-Meda, 2016). And, when possible, training should include both the transfer of knowledge (the more traditional approach to training) and professional co-development that emphasizes breakout groups, case studies, interactive exercises, affinity groups, peer mentoring, consultation clinics, and the like (Gandhi & Johnson, 2016). Young and her colleagues (2022) aptly note:

> When a comprehensive look at what good mentoring entails is coupled with facilitated discussions that encourage mentors to share experiences they have lived or witnessed, mentor training can lean away from "mentoring 101" and benefit both new and more experienced mentors.
>
> (p. 125)

Scant examples of university-led site supervisor training efforts exist—it could be said that there is a gap in translating our knowledge about what makes a good mentor into training programs for internship site supervisors. A notable exception takes us back 25 years to the work of Belle Alderman at the University of Canberra in Australia. As an Associate Professor in Children's Literature in the Division of Communication and Education, Alderman and her colleagues developed an internship program—Partners in Learning (PAL)—for students in the Library and Information Sciences program (Alderman & Milne, 1998). Extensive preparation for supervisors/mentors was a cornerstone of the PAL program. Mentors completed a half-day training during which the goal was to ensure that the university and mentors had a shared vision for students' internship placements. Supervisors learned about Library and Information Science course content and structure in the hopes that they would be better able to help students make links between what is learned in the classroom and real-world situations. During the training, supervisors also met with their assigned interns and crafted what was referred to as a Plan of Learning Experiences—a document that listed student learning goals and objectives and the concrete steps supervisors would take to mentor and support students. These plans were reviewed and approved by PAL program staff and faculty.

Training and support for supervisors involved in the PAL program continued after the half-day training. After the first two weeks of the internship, a university academic advisor met with students and mentors at the internship sites to "discuss progress, clarify matters, and ensure the environment is contributing to the student's learning . . . These meetings enable the academic supervisor to identify potential problems and to foster the collaborative nature of the internship" (Alderman & Milne, 1998, p. 233). Finally, all parties (i.e., interns, supervisors, and program staff) engaged in reflection on the experience. Staff utilized this opportunity to evaluate and make modifications to student and mentor training and evaluate the quality of mentors. Feedback from students and mentors about their experiences was considered for future placements.

While comprehensive and laudable, the PAL program training is best characterized as traditional in that much of it involves knowledge transfer in the form of sharing information with mentors about program expectations and best practices in mentoring. Lamentably, ongoing opportunities for site supervisors to come together to share information and resources or problem solve were missing. Further, the mentor training (and the program) required a sizable resource and time commitment from the university and the mentors, something that may not be replicable or sustainable over time. Nevertheless, the PAL program provides an adaptable model for certain campuses under certain circumstances. At the very least, nobody could argue that more scaffolding is disadvantageous.

In the quest to identify other options for offering internship site supervisor training that do not require as much time or resources (but are still effective), we might look to mentor training offered as part of other high-impact experiences on university campuses. One example is the Advancing Inclusive Mentoring (AIM) program created at California State University, Long Beach for faculty members who work with undergraduate and graduate students on independent research, scholarly, or creative works (Young et al., 2022). This training program includes both the transfer of knowledge (i.e., best practices in inclusive and positive mentoring) and the opportunity for mentors to interact, discuss best practices in mentoring, and learn from each other. An advantage of the AIM program is that it does not require a major time or resource investment for program staff overseeing the training. Mentors engage asynchronously with online videos grouped into six modules: Communicating with Your Mentees, Inclusive Mentoring, Mentee Growth and Development, Mentee Health and Wellbeing, Mentee-Centered Mentoring, and a Mentoring Toolbox. Each module is about 40 minutes in length. The Inclusive Mentoring module is noteworthy in that it addresses a range of topics for building skills critical for serving diverse and underrepresented students: the importance of equity and inclusion, understanding privilege, unconscious bias, managing microaggressions, confronting discrimination, and culturally aware mentoring (Young et al., 2022). The post-viewing activities have faculty participate in facilitated discussions where all participants can share their own experiences, ask questions, react to the mentoring scenarios presented in the videos, and help each other solve prevalent mentoring challenges.

Young et al.'s (2022) assessment of the program demonstrates the power of facilitated discussions. Additionally, "most participants reported being 'Extremely Likely' to make changes to their mentoring practices because of this training" (p. 120). This is noteworthy, as trainings are effective only if what is learned is transferred from the training environment to interactions with one's mentee. This represents a challenge, not just in mentor training, but across organizations that provide training to employees as means for improving skills, increasing knowledge, and shifting attitudes. In other words, just because we train people, does not mean they will use the information to inform their behaviors. Hughes et al. (2018) created a checklist that facilitates the transfer of training material into action. Aligning the training with specific objectives (i.e., tailor training—one size does not fit all), facilitating a climate which encourages learning, supporting the use of trained skills after the training (i.e., not a one-and-done training event), providing feedback to mentors, and updating training materials as needed are part of its objectives (Hughes et al., 2018).

In some disciplines, professional organizations have developed training materials (e.g., videos and handbooks) for their own constituents that are easily accessible when supervisors need ideas and direction. A guide developed by the American Institute of Architects (2012) for their Intern Development Program (IDP), a structured transition program from formal higher education to careers in architecture administered by the National Council of Architectural Registration Board (NCARB), figures as a salient one. *Mentoring Essentials* (American Institute of Architects, 2012) addresses a range of topics including characteristics of formal mentoring, the history of mentoring, matching issues, characteristics of sound mentors, characteristics of receptive mentees, benefits to mentors and mentees, responsibilities, tips, advice on giving constructive feedback, direction on setting goals with interns, keeping lines of communication open, and how to bring closure to the match. These training materials represent a feasible alternative to face-to-face trainings when resources like time and staff are in short supply.

In the absence of university or agency commitments to offer site supervisor training or disciplinary-specific training guides, many turn to readily available online materials like manuals and courses that can be accessed as needed (Hamori, 2021). MENTOR, a US-based nonprofit committed to improving mentoring relationships through evidence-based practices, offers their cornerstone publication, *Elements of Effective Practice for Mentoring* (Garringer et al., 2015) and several supplemental briefs (Kupersmidt et al., 2019). These resources impart useful information on recruiting, screening, training, matching, and supporting mentors. MENTOR also holds periodic live webinars that provide information on timely mentoring topics. These webinars are led by MENTOR staff and provide mentors the opportunity to engage in dialogue as well as celebrate mentoring relationship achievements and milestones. Similar resources are provided by the European Mentoring and Coaching Council (2023) which "exists to develop, promote, and set the expectations for best practices in mentoring, coaching and supervision globally for the benefit of society" (para. 1).

Training site supervisors to mentor and support student interns involves many decisions—who to train, what content to include in trainings, and how to deliver the trainings effectively. Each of these decisions represents an opportunity to engage in provocative praxis, to seek the potentially contradictory input of site hosts, students, and university faculty and staff, to challenge the way site supervisor trainings have been done previously (if at all), and to compromise when there are competing agendas (an aspect of the political frame). Multiple approaches to mentor training are likely necessary if site supervisors are to be ready to host our interns in ways that honor students' cultural capital and ensure that internship experiences lead to student learning and success.

Partners as contributors to educational curriculum

In this section, we propose a reconsideration of partners' roles as it relates to curriculum. Rossi-Le (2015) asserts,

> Employers play a vital role in that dialogue as well, evaluating student performance on the job, communicating with internship faculty, and offering insight into the knowledge and skill set future graduates will need to gain a competitive edge in their respective fields.
>
> (p. 3)

We can benefit by having internship site supervisors and industry partners as part of the feedback process to improve student's internship experiences and career readiness for post-graduation opportunities. Curricular partnerships also signal to our community partners that we are committed to developing authentic partnerships that directly engage them in the education and career development process. These organizations will be hiring recent graduates; therefore, educators should be open to listening and adapting internship curriculum that best prepare students for post-graduation employment. Furthermore, having organizations as part of the curricular development helps them better design meaningful tasks and projects to tie into and reflect what is happening in the classroom.

The College of Science at Swansea University (Wales, UK) incorporated employer feedback into their curriculum design, with the goal of minimizing the skills gap between higher education and industry, and to demonstrate that "effective and well-balanced curriculums can be created as provisions can be refined to ensure they both satisfy the academic acquisition of theoretical knowledge while developing career-relevant professional skills" (Roberts et al., 2021, p. 3). Through employer questionnaires and job post analysis, faculty identified new learning outcomes, activities, and assessments that addressed employer requirements while also taking into consideration available university resources. Evaluation of the data resulted in creating two new field course modules, one including work-simulated learning during the students' third year to develop professional skills in ecological conservation. Students completed five work-related learning activities that incorporated subject knowledge, technical, and transferable skills, which employers identified as the most important skill sets of recent graduates. Students completed an evaluation of the field course and 100% of students strongly agreed or agreed that they "enjoyed the field course" and the field course "helped to develop employability skills." The program also invited employers as part of the steering committee to review the course material. This type of circular feedback adds value to all entities involved: students engage in the most up-to-date knowledge, skills, and technology needed to learn employable skills through their degree; programs develop partnerships with local organizations that participate in professional development activities, provide internship and experiential learning opportunities, and partner with organizations to secure joint research and funding opportunities; and employers become active participants in the student-learning process and can impact a students' preparedness for careers while simultaneously (and serendipitously) identifying potential talent for their organizations (Roberts et al., 2021).

While some faculty and administrators may welcome an organization's input, others may resist, insisting that curriculum is exclusively the teacher's domain. This type of partnership works well for more technical degrees, such as the example above at Swansea University, where there tends to be a direct major to market connection, but its applicability to liberal arts degrees, may prove more challenging (Roberts et al., 2021). Often faculty feel they "own" the curriculum, perhaps because it is the one area where they feel they have real autonomy and influence. Many faculty take offense when employers try to tell them what they should be teaching in the classroom, and insistence exacerbates the tension surrounding the vocational school versus university debate. In effect, many faculty claim that their role is to teach critical thinking and mastery of disciplinary content, not work-based skills. We have heard them ask "Isn't that the role of the community colleges or the Career Development Center?" Busteed (2019) puts the debate into perspective:

> What would you rather have a graduate who is broadly educated and prepared for any number of jobs as a critical thinker, skilled communicator, etc., or a grad who has work experience and hard skills? The correct answer is neither. It's both. And there's no reason—other than ignorance, snobbish attitudes and a lack of creativity and new elbow-grease put into pedagogical design—that we can't have both at the same time, in the same graduate.
>
> (para. 4)

This, then, becomes an issue of reeducating faculty to be in tune with students' needs and incorporating the research that greenlights collaborative efforts between faculty and internship-sponsoring organizations.

So, what happens when faculty and departments are unwilling to yield control or bring partnering organizations into the fold? Companies may decide to create or redesign educational programs to meet their employment needs. Then faculty will have to decide what they are willing to sacrifice: some intellectual control with partners or all of it with companies. In Busteed's

(2020) *Forbes* article, he cites three examples of donor-sponsored activities, or organizations acquiring programs to meet their hiring needs. State Farm donated $30 million to Arizona State University to provide scholarships to high school, community college students, and working adults to fund pathways toward four-year degrees. Facing a potential pilot shortage, United Airlines acquired Westwind School of Aeronautics, creating its own Aviate Academy to meet demands. The Dallas Cowboys partnered with the University of North Texas to create a new online MBA in Sports Entertainment Management (Busteed, 2020). This may well be the future of integrated education: The perception that students' education will be more industry focused, thus preparing them better for career opportunities. If universities want to be proactive, versus reactive, to industry needs and to holistically prepare students for post-graduation employment, then we need to be amenable to prototype and collaborate with industry partners to create valuable learning opportunities that enhance students' educational experiences. Education is always evolving, as the integration of AI attests, and we can either resist or adapt.

Internship programs beyond the university

Perhaps we (universities) do not need to go this alone. Can we direct students to established entities that can fill the gap where the university is not able to meet students' needs once vetted? For example, California Intern Network, operated by University Enterprises, Inc., a non-profit, auxiliary organization serving California State University, offers paid, part-time internship opportunities for undergraduate, graduate, and international students to intern in California state agencies (University Enterprises Inc., 2023). They connect students to internships within government agencies, which can be a complicated application and hiring process. Other well-established internship programs, such as INROADS, who offer paid internships and a focus on diversity, equity, and inclusion, already have strong partnerships with corporations (INROADS Inc., 2021). In 2021, Henkel (the company behind well-known brands such as Dial®, Right Guard®, and Persil®) dedicated an initial $600,000 investment to scholarships and internship programs in the United States, Canada, and Puerto Rico to increase diversity, equity, and inclusion across Henkel businesses. Henkel has partnered with INROADS and CEE Centre For Young Black Professionals to host paid student interns at their businesses (Henkel, 2021). For students to participate in these opportunities, we need to make stronger connections with organizations like INROADS, which can create a bridge for students to access high quality, paid internships. Student interns also work with INROADS advisors to receive professional development training and coaching, preparing them for the internship experience and beyond. Developing partnerships with established internship programs can increase access to opportunities, lessen the workload for faculty and staff, and shore up resources. Instead of sourcing and creating opportunities, faculty and staff can focus on preparing students and referring a pipeline of talent from the university to these programs.

The prospect of paid internships with these sorts of organizations for Students of Color is an additional draw. Businesses and local workforce and economic development offices boast innovative partnerships to increase paid internships to historically underserved populations. Starting in 2020, the Michigan Founders Fund (MFF, formally the A2 Entrepreneurs Fund), launched their Diversity, Equity & Inclusion Internship Program, which specifically focuses on addressing the lack of diversity and representation in the tech and start-up industries (Business Wire, 2022). This internship program is a collaborative effort of local colleges, community organizations, and startup venture capital firms, each contributing staff time and/or money to launch the program. To bolster partnerships, an MFF-lead advisory team consisting of program sponsor Bank of Ann Arbor, community organizations, the Ann Arbor Area Community Foundation and Detroit Promise, and participating colleges, Washtenaw Community College, Eastern Michigan University, and University of Michigan-Dearborn, meet as a committee to select applicants for each cohort. In 2022, MFF placed 16 student interns at 11 Michigan-based tech companies. Now in its third year, Trista Van Tine (Business Wire, 2022), Executive Director of MMF shares:

> Michigan's high-growth sector continues to experience healthy growth, but the talent within the community is often disproportionate to the diversity found across the state. The Future Founders Internship Program is one step in efforts to change this trajectory as we provide internships, training, and mentorship to diverse Michigan college students while also helping tech startups develop or strengthen their diversity, equity, and inclusion initiatives and reach new talent.
>
> (para. 3)

In a similar vein, the internship program addresses the representation issue as well. Data show that program interns self-identify as "75% women, nonbinary, or gender nonconforming, 81% Black, Indigenous, or People of Color, 56% are PELL-eligible, and 44% are part of the LGBTQ community" (Business Wire, 2022, para. 1).

Beyond merely cultivating opportunities, MFF strives to incorporate foundational elements of internships into the experience. Student interns receive skill development workshops, professional mentorship, and networking opportunities with their cohort as well as professionals from participating organizations. Not only do students receive training but also all participating organizations are required to complete three EDIA-focused workshops and consultations lead by Thrive and Shine LLC (Business Wire, 2022). MFF understands the importance of recruiting diverse talent as well as making sure organizations are prepared to receive and mentor diverse talent. The popularity of the program shows in the numbers: student applications doubled within one year to 140 for 16 positions. This is a testament to programs like The Future Founders Internship Program, and scaling and/or replicating them is just one effective way to meet student needs.

Benefits to partnering organizations and supervisors

This chapter has focused primarily on the logistics of partnering with community organizations to provide host site mentoring and supervision for interns by interrogating the how (to cultivate authentic partnerships) and the what (training for supervisors might look like to maximize student interns benefit burden). We would be remiss if we did not acknowledge that authentic partnerships between host sites and universities can benefit partnering organizations and supervisors in ways that transcend the obvious. In effect, internship placements can be arrangements that are beneficial to all involved—students, hosting agencies, and the university (see Chapter 1 for a discussion of mutualism).

At the organizational level, hosting interns provides a relatively low-cost means for screening and recruiting potential hires, especially as there is no inherent expectation of future employment when hosting interns (McHugh, 2017). If companies are serious about fostering diverse workforces, internships, especially those that are paid, can help ensure that students from a broad spectrum of backgrounds (including Students of Color) with fresh perspectives will apply (Rockwood, 2020). In effect, securing ongoing internship placements "builds talent pipelines and provides access to students who are often excluded from traditional recruiting" (Tu & Li, 2021, p. 2). Further, evidence from NACE's (2011) Internship and Co-Op Report suggests that hosting interns who are eventually hired boosts company retention rates. That is, employees who previously interned with the organization are more likely to be retained at both the one-year and five-year marks than hires who interned somewhere else and hires with no internship experience.

Internships can also build a company's brand and name recognition on university campuses and in the region. Students who have positive internship experiences with an organization are likely to share their experiences (and perspectives) with their classmates which can translate to recruitment of additional interns for the company and positive perceptions of the company overall. As Willison (2012) notes, "Creating an internship program is an excellent way to give back . . . Hiring students not only helps students in your community get started, it enhances the local workforce as a whole" (p. 351).

Employees also benefit personally and professionally from supervising student interns if they approach the task from a place of reciprocity and believe that there is something to learn from their interns (Jeske & Linehan, 2020). Zhang et al. (2023) explain that:

> When mentors adopt a downward learning direction, or the belief that individuals below them in positional power are valuable sources of their learning, they become more effective mentors, both objectively and subjectively. A downward learning direction transformed mentoring from a costly obligation into a learning opportunity, leading mentors to become more engaged and to ultimately improve the learning experiences and outcomes of their mentees.
>
> (p. 630)

Supervisors who are open to crafting mutually beneficial relationships with their interns can gain personal satisfaction from mentoring emerging professionals, experience the synergy of partnering with an intern on a project, develop a better understanding of younger workers and an awareness of issues in the field, and improve their leadership skills (Reeves, 2022). The benefits conferred to potential supervisors may be especially helpful for those who have limited managerial or delegation experience. Supervisors who "successfully mentor interns will be better equipped to manage and train employees in the future, which can have a positive impact on employee retention and engagement levels" (Reeves, 2022, para. 18).

By bringing community partners into the fold, we aim to dismantle the fragmented mentality and silos that often befall college internship programs. Authentic partnerships with agencies and organizations that mentor and support our student interns begin by promoting interactions grounded in negotiation. In this way, we encourage stakeholders—including community partners, students, and campus administrators, staff and faculty—to build programs and provide training that enlightens through provocation.

References

Alderman, B., & Milne, P. (1998). Partners in learning—educators, practitioners and students collaborate on work-based learning—a case study. *Higher Education Research & Development, 17*(2), 229–238. https://doi.org/10.1080/0729436980170207

American Institute of Architects. (2012). *Mentoring essentials for IDP supervisors and mentors*. aia-mentoring-essentials-idp.pdf (emfp.org)

Bhattacharya, S., & Neelam, N. (2018). Perceived value of internship experience: A try before you leap. *Higher Education, Skills and Work—Based Learning, 8*(4), 376–394. https://doi.org/10.1108/HESWBL-07-2017-0044

Bolman, L. G., & Gallos, J. V. (2011). *Reframing academic leadership*. Jossey-Bass.

Business Wire. (2022). *Michigan Founders Fund: Future founders internship program welcomes underrepresented college talent into the state's startup ecosystem*. www.businesswire.com/news/home/20220613005027/en/

Busteed, B. (2019). Why college will soon be about credegrees and co-ops. *Forbes.* forbes.com

Busteed, B. (2020). "Employer U" is here, and it's here to stay. *Forbes.* forbes.com

California Competes. (2022, July). *Barriers & opportunities for building higher education–employer partnerships.* Employer-Engagement-Brief-Final.pdf (californiacompetes.org)

Cho, C. S., Ramanan, R. A., & Feldman, M. D. (2011). Defining the ideal qualities of mentorship: A qualitative analysis of the characteristics of outstanding mentors. *The American Journal of Medicine, 124*(5), 453–458. https://doi.org/10.1016/j.amjmed.2010.12.007

Crawford, P., & Fink, W. (2020, June). *From academia to the workforce: Executive summary.* Association of Public & Land-Grant Universities. from-academia-to-the-workforce-executive-summary.pdf (aplu.org)

D'Abate, C. P., Youndt, M. A., & Wenzel, K. E. (2009). Making the most of an internship: An empirical study of internship satisfaction. *Academy of Management Learning & Education, 8*(4), 527–539. https://doi.org/10.5465/AMLE.2009.47785471

Ensher, E. A., Grant-Vallone, E. J., & Marelich, W. D. (2002). Effects of perceived attitudinal and demographic similarity on protégés' support and satisfaction gained from their mentoring relationships. *Journal of Applied Social Psychology, 32*(7), 1407–1430. https://doi.org/10.1111/j.1559-1816.2002.tb01444.x

European Mentoring and Coaching Council. (2023). *Our purpose.* www.emccglobal.org/

Gandhi, M., & Johnson, M. (2016). Creating more effective mentors: Mentoring the mentor. *AIDS and Behavior, 20*(2), 294–303. https://doi.org/10.1007/s10461-016-1364-3

Garringer, M., Kupersmidt, J., Rhodes, J., Stelter, R., & Tai, T. (2015). *Elements of effective practice for mentoring.* MENTOR/National Mentoring Partnership.

Gray, K. (2021, April 6). *Overcoming obstacles: Managing internships in a one-person URR office.* National Association of Colleges and Employers. naceweb.org

Hamori, M. (2021). MOOCs at work: What induces employer support for them? *The International Journal of Human Resource Management, 32*(20), 4190–4214. https://doi.org/10.1080/09585192.2019.1616593

Henkel. (2021, March 3). *Henkel North America announces new DEI scholarship and internship programs.* https://www.henkel.com/press-and-media/press-releases-and-kits/2021-03-03-henkel-north-america-announces-new-scholarship-and-internship-programs-1155924

Hora, M., Chen, Z., Parrott, E., & Her, P. (2020). Problematizing college internships: Exploring issues with access, program design, and developmental outcomes. *International Journal of Work-Integrated Learning, 21*(3), 235–252.

Hora, M., Wolfgram, M., Chen, Z., Zhang, J., & Fischer, J. J. (2020). *A sociocultural analysis of internship supervision: Insights from a mixed-methods study of interns at five postsecondary institutions* (WCER Working Paper No. 20208). University of Wisconsin-Madison, Wisconsin Center for Education Research. www.wcer.wisc.edu/publications/working-papers-no-2020-8

Hughes, A. M., Zajac, S., Spencer, J. H., & Salas, E. (2018). A checklist for facilitating training transfer in organizations. *International Journal of Training and Development, 22*(4), 334–345. https://doi.org/10.1111/ijtd.12141

INROADS Inc. (2021). *What is the INROADS internship program?* https://inroads.org/internships-program/

Jeske, D., & Linehan, C. (2020). Mentoring and skill development in e-Internships. *Journal of Work-Applied Management*, *12*(2), 245–258. https://doi.org/10.1108/JWAM-

Kupersmidt, J., Stelter, R., Garringer, M., & Mayhew, J. (2019). *Workplace mentoring: Supplement to elements of effective practice for mentoring*. Mentor.

Lave, J., & Wenger, E. (1991). *Situated learning: Legitimate peripheral participation*. Cambridge University Press. https://doi.org/10.1017/CBO9780511815355

Lockwood, P. (2006). Someone like me can be successful: Do college students need same-gender role models? *Psychology of Women Quarterly*, *30*(1), 36–46. https://doi.org/10.1111/j.1471-6402.2006.00260.x

Lopes, B., Silva, P., Melo, A. I., Brito, E., Paiva Días, G., & Costa, M. (2019). The 'lunar side' of the story: Exploring the sustainability of curricular internships in higher education. *Sustainability*, *11*(21), 1–22. https://doi.org/10.3390/su11215879

Luedke, C. L. (2017). Person first, student second: Staff and administrators of color supporting students of color authentically in higher education. *Journal of College Student Development*, *58*(1), 37–52. https://doi.org/10.1353/csd.2017.0002

Luedke, C. L., Collom, G. D., & Henderson, T. N. (2023). Developing a culture of mentoring: Promoting, experiencing, and engaging in mentoring through a transitional undergraduate research program for students of color. *Mentoring & Tutoring: Partnership in Learning*, *31*(1), 39–60. https://doi.org/10.1080/13611267.2023.2164991

McCoy, D. L., Winkle-Wagner, R., & Luedke, C. L. (2015). Colorblind mentoring? Exploring white faculty mentoring of students of color. *Journal of Diversity in Higher Education*, *8*(4), 225–242. https://doi.org/10.1037/a0038676

McHugh, P. P. (2017). The impact of compensation, supervision and work design on internship efficacy: Implications for educators, employers and prospective interns. *Journal of Education and Work*, *30*(4), 367–382. https://doi.org/10.1080/1363908 0.2016.1181729

National Association of Colleges and Employers. (2011). *Internship & co-op report*. www.naceweb.org/store/2023/internship-and-co-op-report/

Neelam, N., Bhattacharya, S., Kejriwal, V., Bhardwaj, V., Goyal, A., Saxena, A., Dhawan, D., Vaddi, A., & Choudaha, G. (2019). Internship in a business school: Expectation versus experience. *Higher Education, Skills, and Work-Based Learning*, *9*(1), 92–106. https://doi.org/10.1108/HESWBL-03-2018-0025

Reeves, M. (2022). Mentoring interns: Helping future top talent grow. *Together Newsletter*. Together Mentoring Software (togetherplatform.com)

Roberts, L. J., Neyland, P. J., Devine, A. P., Harris, W. E., Bull, J. C., Froyd, C. A., Eastwood, D. C., Forman, D. W., & Elias, O. H. (2021). You said, we did! Employer led work-simulated learning framework for enhancing ecology graduate employability. *Journal of Biological Education*, 1–20. https://doi.org/10.1080/00219266.2021.197 9624

Rockwood, K. (2020). How a well-planned internship program can benefit your organization. *HR Magazine*, (Spring), 1. shrm.org

Rossi-Le, L. (2015). Provide access to internships across the college curriculum. *Dean and Provost*, *16*(7), 1–3. https://doi.org/10.1002/dap.30033

Santos, S. J., & Reigadas, E. T. (2002). Latinos in higher education: An evaluation of a university faculty mentoring program. *Journal of Hispanic Higher Education*, *1*(1), 40–50. https://doi.org/10.1177/1538192702001001004

Spiekermann, L., Lawrence, E., Lyons, M., & Deutsch, N. (2021). A qualitative analysis of the utility of a competency framework for mentor training. *Mentoring & Tutoring:*

Partnership in Learning, 29(5), 565–585. https://doi.org/10.1080/13611267.2021.1986793

St-Jean, É., & Mitrano-Meda, S. (2016). Should mentors of entrepreneurs be trained or their experience is enough? In M. Franco (Ed.), *Entrepreneurship: Practice-oriented perspectives* (pp. 39–61). IntechOpen. https://doi.org/10.5772/65625

Tu, M., & Li, M. (2021). What great mentorship looks like in a hybrid workplace. *Harvard Business Review.* https://hbr.org/2021/05/what-great-mentorship-looks-?autocomplete=true

University Enterprises Inc. (2023). *California intern network.* https://calinterns.org/

Willison, S. (2012). How internship programs benefit employers. *Strategic HR Review, 11*(6). https://doi.org/10.1108/shr.2012.37211faa.008

Yosso, T. J. (2005). Whose culture has capital? A critical race theory discussion of community cultural wealth. *Race Ethnicity and Education, 8*(1), 69–91. https://doi.org/10.1080/1361332052000341006

Young, K. A., Marayong. P., & Vu, K-P. L. (2022). Faculty mentor training to change mentoring practices at a diverse R2 university. *Journal on Excellence in College Teaching, 33*(4), 105–132.

Zhang, T., Wang, D., & Galinsky, A. D. (2023). Learning down to train up: Mentors are more effective when they value insights from below. *Academy of Management Journal, 6*(2), 604–637. https://doi.org//10.5465/amj.2021.0430

5 Assessment as a Catalyst for Addressing Equity in Internships

> We will not deliver on the promise of HIPs [including internships], least of all their potential for driving equity, without simultaneously attending to the questions of fidelity, scale, and assessment.
>
> (Zilvinskis et al., 2022, p. 6)

Despite a longstanding history of assessment in higher education, or what some refer to as an obsession (e.g., Worthen, 2018), assessing high-impact practices like internships is relatively new. Finley (2019) contends that, "the biggest impediment to assessing high-impact practices may very well be the name itself. The term, 'high-impact,' almost *assumes* efficacy. With a name like that, what is left to assess? The answer is plenty" (p. 4). In this chapter, we take a critical look at several components of internship assessment including where to start, what to assess, how to identify and collect assessment data, and who will do the work. We also address data analytic strategies that have the greatest potential to expose equity gaps in internship participation and student outcomes and lead to more inclusive internship programming.

Throughout the chapter, we turn to the work of Ashley Finely, Jillian Kinzie, Matthew Hora, and John Zilvinskis, experts in HIPs assessment, to inform our discussions. We draw examples and inspiration from Zilvinkis et al.'s (2022) recently published book, *Delivering on the Promise of High-Impact Practices: Research and Models for Achieving Equity, Fidelity, Impact and Scale*. We also highlight local examples of assessment, including the multi-disciplinary, multi-method assessment of internships conducted by faculty at California State University, Long Beach (HIPs@the Beach).

Where to start and what to assess

Knowing where to begin can be overwhelming, especially when assessment is an afterthought or done simply to comply with internal mandates or accreditation guidelines. Finley et al. (2022) contend that:

> The starting point for assessing equity-centered HIPs demands the articulation of a vision for the practices that conceptualizes why equity matters

DOI: 10.4324/9781003296324-5

for the future of the institution, for students' lives, and for standards of excellence . . . the outcomes chosen to operationalize the effects of HIPs on students' learning and development should, themselves, have echoes in the vision.

(p. 25)

Perhaps the most useful vision statements situate internship programming and corresponding initiatives in the larger context of university priorities for student learning and success and focus on expected changes to student behavior and knowledge. As an example, our campus has been engaged in a campus-wide strategic planning process (i.e., Beach 2030) meant to identify innovative modes of operation, garner buy-in, and promote a shared understanding, clarity, and culture around the future of our university. One of the resulting strategic priorities of Beach 2030 is to "prepare students for their journeys to success in a fast-changing world with a rapidly shifting economy and labor market" (CSULB University Strategic Communications, 2021, p. 13). This includes engaging students in robust professional internships, preparing students to think critically and problem-solve, offering students opportunities to hone life skills, and committing to students' socioeconomic mobility. California State University, Long Beach's newly launched campus-wide Academic Internships Office has aligned its vision for academic internships with this campus-wide strategic priority. That is, the office is committed to ensuring equitable access to and participation in paid internships for all students that honor the cultural assets that students bring to campus and provide opportunities for students to clarify career goals, hone professional skills, and experience personal growth (Yosso, 2005). Importantly, this vision statement points to critical areas of assessment including the tracking of who does (and does not) have ready access to paid internship opportunities and the identification of students' cultural assets and the ways they are recognized (or not) in our internship programs. The vision statement also calls attention to the outcomes—the learning (i.e., knowledge and skills) and personal growth (e.g., increased self-confidence)—we expect students to experience as a result of participating in high-quality academic internships.

Aligning vision statements for internship programming with articulated university priorities is, however, not without risk. University mission statements and corresponding strategic priorities can be full of buzzwords and marketing language that sound impressive but bear little resemblance to how campuses actually operate. In other words, there can be a lot of "talk" but relatively little "walk" resulting in nothing more than the symbolic framing of good intentions. If your internship vision (and assessment practices) misaligns with campus priorities, you may find yourself frustrated and under resourced as you tackle the hard work of internship programming and assessment. Further, campuses typically have multiple priorities, yet limited resources. It is important to know which priorities are currently taking precedence as campus

Assessment as a Catalyst for Addressing Equity in Internships 91

activities that are aligned with them may be the only ones publicly recognized and resourced.

Launching an intentional and meaningful assessment of internships also demands a clear sense of what is being offered by way of academic internship programming across your campus. Finley (2019) refers to this as taking an inventory or asset mapping. This would include identifying the various academic internship courses being offered, internship programs that provide comprehensive support and coaching, and companies and organizations that routinely host student interns. This could also include an inventory of where the internship resources are positioned on campus (some colleges may have resources like staff and funding whereas others do not) and who is collecting internship assessment data which would be helpful in determining if there is any unnecessary duplication. Being able to map the internship opportunities available to students is the first step in tracking which students are completing internships and where equitable access is lacking.

The myriad ways internships are operationalized and labeled complicate the practice of conducting an inventory of academic internships. That is, internships often are called different things (e.g., practica, fieldwork, clinical placements, apprenticeship, etc.) and are organized according to discipline-specific norms, thereby making it difficult to get consensus on what, in fact, constitutes an internship. In addition, departments that track internship participation often do so only for credit-bearing internships. Students who complete internships on their own (non-credit experiences) typically do so without informing their home departments; these internships are thus less likely to be tracked by universities. A notable exception is Shippensburg University (2023) which encourages students to register (via an online portal) internship opportunities that are not completed for credit and do not count towards degree completion. By registering their non-credit internships, students receive recognition from the Career, Mentoring, and Professional Development Center (Shippensburg University, 2023).

Further complicating the process of inventorying internships is the need for an online platform or software (and staff dedicated to maintaining it over time) that can be costly. Organizations like Student Opportunity Center (a People Grove company) are dedicated to helping universities audit their existing experiential opportunities including internships and then implementing customized plans that include assessing student learning, operationalizing equity goals, and building a robust data infrastructure. More localized online tracking platforms can cost less but provide less customization and fewer services. As an example, we currently use CalState S4 on our campus, an integrated web application that allows us to facilitate student placements and track student participation (completed hours) for a range of experiential learning activities including internships. Students, community host sites, and our campus have access to the S4 platform allowing all stakeholders to track students' participation. Regardless of which platform or software universities decide to use, faculty and staff buy-in for using it is important, otherwise, it can be difficult to get a comprehensive overview of internships on campus.

Despite the benefits of conducting an inventory prior to launching new internship programs or conducting assessments, campus administrators have been known to resist mapping academic internship opportunities and resources. Why is unclear. While it could be the cost and time associated with completing an inventory, it seems something more may be fueling the resistance, a belief perhaps that experiential learning activities like internships are extracurricular or nonacademic and thus do not warrant a data-driven approach. We disagree and urge campuses to invest in asset mapping as a necessary first step to ensuring equitable access to and participation in academic internships.

Knowing what internship opportunities exist, who completes them, and the total number of hours worked though is just the first step, for it tells us nothing about why some students do not participate in academic internships (the barriers to participating), the quality of academic internship experiences, student satisfaction, or the ideal timing of these experiences. As Kinzie, McCormick et al. (2021) urge, we must get beyond labeling something as a high-impact practice and assuming all students experience them positively, to measuring students' exposure to the elements of high-impact experiences (e.g., opportunities to reflect and connect coursework to real-world situations) and student learning gains like problem-solving and leadership abilities. Students' perceptions of their internship experiences—the type of work they completed, their ability to network with professionals in their fields, and the skills honed—are critical for understanding the immediate and long-term value of internships to students' post-graduation success. Further, if we expect equitable access to and participation in internships to result in social mobility, increased sense of belonging, greater retention rates, and post-graduation employment, then we need to include these outcomes in our assessment plans. Asking tough questions about how our internship courses and programs are delivered—an issue of fidelity—is also central to the assessment process as implementation can vary considerably even within the same college and department. Finley et al. (2022) argue that:

> Because quality of implementation is often assumed rather than intentionally assessed, it can be the Achilles' heel of outcome results. Without implementation of the aspects of HIPs that actually make them high impact, hypothesized effects on outcomes can fall apart or, at the very least, are far less assured.
>
> (p. 25)

How to assess students' internship experiences

Even when we can decide what is worth tracking and measuring, we often spend an inordinate amount of time identifying the "best method" for assessing internships, as if a single approach could adequately capture the complexities of these potentially transformative experiences. We instead advocate for options, including the use of multiple methods including national and local surveys, focus groups, interviews, and students' photos and narratives, while simultaneously calling for the re-distribution of power in ways that recognize students as experts on their own experiences (relevant to both the human resource and political frames).

The *Assessing Quality and Equity in High-Impact Practices* project, funded by the Lumina Foundation and launched by Indiana University's Center for Postsecondary Research, represents the first systematic and national attempt to assess the degree to which internships and other HIPs deliver on the eight elements that qualify HIPs as transformative (Kinzie et al., 2020). This project incorporated data from over 50 bachelor's-degree-granting institutions to develop the HIPs Quality Assessment Tool. Once refined, this tool was appended to the National Survey of Student Engagement (NSSE) of first-year students and seniors and fashioned into a standalone survey that can be deployed by individual campuses for a nominal fee. Over 20,000 students completed the initial 40-question survey, of which almost 6,000 had finished an internship (Kinzie et al., 2020).

The purported advantage of the HIPs Quality Assessment Tool is the ability to use NSSE findings as benchmarks to analyze local data collected via the same tool. For example, initial findings using the tool indicate that 81% of students who completed internships reported that they applied the theory learned in their coursework to real-world problems (Kinzie et al., 2020). A recent assessment of one of our campus-wide paid internship programs reveals that 87% of our student interns reported putting theory into practice at their sites, suggesting our internship program is on par with other programs across the country in terms of this defining element of HIPs. Imagine though if we had fallen short of the 81% benchmark. In this instance, we would have been prompted to inquire why our students were not given opportunities to apply theory to real-world problems and then possibly to engage in program improvement, curriculum development, and supplemental internship site and faculty trainings.

Despite its appeal, we question the utility of the HIPs Quality Assessment Tool as a relevant benchmark for quality for all campuses, as it may privilege whiteness as the normalized frame. Although efforts were made to incorporate a diverse group of students when developing the HIPs Quality Assessment Tool, almost 70% of students who completed surveys and answered questions about their internship placements self-identified as white, and only a quarter were first-generation college students (Kinzie et al., 2020). These demographics differ substantially from campuses that identify as Hispanic-serving, AAPI-serving, or historically Black. Might students at more diverse campuses experience internships differently, either for the better or worse?

To better understand participation gaps among racially minoritized students (and perhaps in response to some skepticism about the utility of the

HIPs Quality Assessment Tool as a benchmark for more diverse campuses), Kinzie, Silberstein, et al. (2021) analyzed survey responses from Students of Color to open-ended prompts about the most and least satisfying aspects of HIPs experiences. The content analysis of students' responses was guided by Yosso's (2005) community cultural wealth model and focused on the links between students' cultural assets and HIPs experiences. Kinzie, Silberstein and their colleagues (2021) report that "racially minoritized students highlight how they were required to balance multiple projects and obligations simultaneously" (p. 10). This is something we have seen in our own assessments of student interns' experiences—family obligations, other paid employment, and heavy courseloads—that require students to expend their navigational capital to successfully traverse what can often be unsupportive contexts and overwhelming expectations. Kinzie, Silberstein, et al. (2021) also found evidence of resistance capital (i.e., challenging the status quo and pursuing equal rights) when students mentioned how they dealt with microaggressions and discriminatory practices during the completion of HIPs.

Possibly the most valuable contribution of Kinzie, Silberstein, et al.'s (2021) content analysis of students' responses to open-ended prompts was the identification of two emerging dimensions of HIPs quality grounded in Students of Color's experiences: an increased sense of agency/accomplishment and the experience of making a difference for others. Again, we can draw corollaries to our own assessment practices where students were also asked to comment on the most satisfying aspects of their internship experiences. The most common themes were having an impact on the local community (e.g., *The most satisfying aspect was having the opportunity to support and feed our elderly citizens and let them know they are appreciated*) and that of increased self-confidence (e.g., *The most satisfying aspect was realizing that I am capable of so much more than I thought. My internship increased my self-confidence and leadership skills. I now feel so much better equipped for future employment/careers*).

Another national survey gaining traction is the National Survey of College Internships (NSCI, 2023), launched by Matthew Hora at the Center for Research on College-Workforce Transitions (CCWT) at the University of Wisconsin. This annual survey is now housed and managed by the Strada Education Network, a nonprofit social impact organization with a mission to improve lives by forging clear and purposeful pathways between education and employment (Strada Education Foundation, 2023). What makes this 58-item survey unique is its singular focus on undergraduate internships (rather than a range of HIPs) and the inclusion of both students who did and did not complete internships, making it possible to identify barriers to access and participation like heavy courseloads and insufficient pay (Hora, 2022). Questions on the survey address internship structure, access, and outcomes. A major benefit to participating in the NSCI though is the access granted to password-protected interactive Tableau data dashboards that include the ability to disaggregate data by gender, race, and class standing, and to download data for more detailed exploration. Participating campuses also receive a set of summary reports and comparisons to a nationally representative benchmark study. Inclusion in the annual survey does, however, comes at a cost of several thousand dollars annually and the commitment of a campus staff person to recruit students to complete the survey, both of which could prevent interested campuses with limited funding and staffing from participating. Additionally, although a few questions address elements of high-quality HIPs, such as ongoing supervisor feedback and the opportunity to learn through real-world application, the survey lamentably overlooks other elements like opportunities to interact with faculty and peers, engagement with diversity, or reflection and integration of learning (National Survey of College Internships, 2023).

Despite our best intentions, it is not enough to participate in or consult national surveys. Comprehensive internship assessment requires several evaluation touch points over time using multiple data sources that promote conversations among stakeholders. Finley (2019) aptly notes that:

> The best outputs for high-impact practices will strike a balance between indirect and direct sources of evidence to ensure no one source of data (and its inherent methodological caveats) overly guide decision-making. Multiple data sources will also ensure multiple opportunities for disaggregating data (of any type) across student populations to assess for equity gaps and related strategies for improvement.
>
> (p. 10)

To fully understand how internships are experienced by students on a campus, it is important to engage in a range of qualitative and quantitative assessment efforts—surveys, focus groups, interviews, and the use of students' photos and narratives—that have been tailored to local contexts.

We refer to HIPs@the Beach (a California State University, Long Beach project) as an illustration of a comprehensive internship assessment that is multi-method, multi-disciplinary, and that amplifies students' voices. Launched in 2020 with the support of the Provost, five faculty members spanning four departments and three colleges collaborated to identify which students on our campus participate in internships, mentored research, and service learning and to better understand the impact of these HIPs on student learning and success. Four sources of assessment data were used in this project as both quantitative and qualitative data are crucial for understanding the experiences of minoritized students, especially as they can reveal why supposed best practices or campus strategies to ensure access are not working for some students.

First, historical student information was retrieved from our Office of Institutional Research and Analytics for all undergraduates who matriculated between 2013 and 2020. This included student demographics, course enrollment information, grades, and time to graduation. Having access to student demographic data allows for the examination of whether and how social identities moderate the effects of internship participation on student success, recognizing that completing internships may be beneficial for some students (but not others) or especially for some students (Kilgo, 2022). Student post-internship surveys and focus groups were also administered. Specifically, the HIPs@the Beach team used the HIPs Quality Assessment Tool to examine student exposure to the elements of high-quality HIPs as well as overall satisfaction. Results suggest that frequency and quality of supervisor feedback are related to greater student learning (e.g., improved problem solving and critical thinking) and overall satisfaction with internship placements. Greater peer collaboration was positively related to greater confidence in leadership skills (Morales et al., 2022). Student focus groups targeted reasons why students participated in internships, experiences with diversity, perceived barriers to participation, internship experiences, and interactions with internship instructors and peers. Focus groups were also held with internship instructors that had been nominated by students as having been helpful and effective. Faculty were asked to discuss their perceptions of the instructor role, how to work with students from diverse backgrounds, how to get students to step out of their comfort zones, and how to develop students' professional identities and aptitudes. Both student and faculty focus groups illuminated systemic barriers to participation in internships as well as the importance of active inclusivity, addressing students' self-limiting beliefs, and creating safe spaces for students to discuss challenges, including those that involve navigating the bridge from college to career (Young et al., 2022).

Photovoice—storytelling through photos and narratives—is an emerging HIPs assessment practice and represents the final source of data collected as part of the HIPs@the Beach project. The goals of Photovoice are to create awareness, give voice to marginalized groups, and to drive change through critical dialogue and sharing (Wang & Burris, 1997). Students who completed internships were asked to take a photo of something that represents the work they completed at their internship sites or the impact that completing an internship had on them. Students were also asked to write a narrative (up to 100 words) explaining their photos. As Figure 5.1 demonstrates, Photovoice is exceptionally effective in capturing outcomes such as sense of belonging, agency, and self-confidence, outcomes that can be difficult or impossible to measure with other assessment methods.

> As a child, I loved school but that love and motivation was replaced with uncertainty as I questioned my choice to stay in school. My internship showed me that no matter how big the task, I can do it and every problem has a solution. I gained confidence in myself through hands-on experiences. I grew professionally and as a person. Most importantly

Assessment as a Catalyst for Addressing Equity in Internships 97

Figure 5.1 Student Photovoice submission reflecting the impact that completing an internship had on them

I rediscovered myself, once again seeing the child in me who loves learning and school and who truly believes the world has endless possibilities and isn't scared to reach for them.

Findings from the HIPs@the Beach project have been presented at national conferences and shared campus wide with faculty and staff who work directly with student interns. We have also used the findings to successfully compel administrators to staff and fund an Academic Internships Office that, among other things, will continue to track and assess the impact of internships on students' learning and success.

An alternative to the indirect assessments detailed above is the use of more direct approaches like assessing student work products. This might look like the application of rating rubrics to student reflection papers, portfolios, and student presentations to their peers and the community indicating what they did, what they learned, and the impact they made (Benedict & Rust, 2016). Direct assessments of student learning require access to and collaboration with faculty teaching internship courses. The goal here, as Kinzie (2020) notes, is to "inspire creativity about what constitutes as a demonstration of achievement" (p. 4). Surveys (both local and national), focus groups, interviews, Photovoice, and more direct assessments like rating student work products all have a place in the assessment of internships and their impact on student learning and personal growth. The challenge is to determine what works for each campus and their students as one size does not fit all. We wonder if there may be benefits to allowing students to choose how they will be assessed. Kinzie (2020) encourages us to cede some of the control over assessment as she notes that, "faculty would do well to offer students agency and encouragement to demonstrate their learning in a format or manner that works best for them" (p. 5).

Identifying who will do the work of assessment

We are keenly aware that our readers may be wondering: But, who will do the work of assessment? Who has time? With systemized planning, it is possible. We challenge assessment being conducted in a fully decentralized manner with uncompensated faculty administering surveys and conducting focus groups and interviews on their own. This approach simply is neither sustainable nor scalable. Further, if each department and unit collect data on their own using internally crafted surveys, for example, aggregating data across the institution becomes impossible, and we are left with disconnected snapshots of internship participation, an incomplete and fragmented picture at best. A better approach is one that fosters collective responsibility for assessment, coordination, and data sharing in a multidirectional move that requires institutional investment in staffing and technology.

Campus-wide councils or committees charged with collecting and examining data are one way to foster a collective responsibility for assessment. Binghamton University's High-Impact Practices Innovations Council (HIPIC) is one example that includes senior administrators as well as staff from across the New York university including people from both academic and student affairs. Interestingly, staff from both University Communications and University Development sit on this council, suggesting there is an explicit university commitment to sharing data widely and funding HIPs like internships. Yousey-Elsener & Pagan (2022) note:

> The ability to track participation data centrally has allowed Binghamton University to explore participation at a higher level than individualized units could achieve on their own. In addition, as a centralized group, HIPIC, brings together campus leadership directors of offices related to each HIP, and the data team to coordinate efforts, ask larger questions, put the data to use, and take steps to increase access.
>
> (p. 217)

A similar collaborative group—the HIPS Infusion Steering Committee—is in place at the Community College of Baltimore County (CCBC). This committee comprised of advisors, faculty, and staff from Enrollment Management and the Office of Research and Evaluation is charged with, among other things, reviewing assessment data (Dolan et al., 2022). The presence and success of this group illustrates that centralized assessment practices are possible at community colleges, not just four-year universities.

Florida State University's Internship Council, which meets at least three times per year to share data and track student engagement, also warrants mention. Their crown jewel figures as a student exit survey instituted as a graduation requirement, which provides information on important student success indicators and participation in experiential learning including internships. Coupled with institutional student information (e.g., demographics, courses taken, etc.):

> These data are assessed and distributed on campus, in institutional performance dashboards for each department and through biannual meetings and briefs with each academic dean. Data are also shared off-campus through promotional materials to students, governing bodies, employers, and others to highlight the university's commitment to student success.
>
> (O'Shea et al., 2022, p. 196)

We recognize that cultivating and supporting centralized committees and councils to oversee the assessment of internships requires a campus-wide commitment and real resources. As an alternative to forming these collaborative groups at the campus level where resources may be lacking, some systems, like the Tennessee Board of Regents (Valentine & Price, 2021), have created system-level groups that collect, review, and disseminate findings about HIPs. Systems have more resources and can leverage across campuses thereby making it easier to provide longitudinal comparisons, amass large sample sizes, break down silos, and disseminate findings widely.

Despite all the aforementioned examples of centralized committees and councils dedicated to assessment, we nevertheless are left wondering, "Where are the student voices?" Rather than the objects of assessment, students can play a pivotal role as facilitators and collaborators. We uphold the idea of training students to assume active roles in internship data collection with their internship-completing peers since the ability to relate as peers may prompt greater disclosure about internship challenges. Similarly, students can also provide valuable insight in the interpretation of data particularly when findings seem counterintuitive. HIPs@the Beach provides an example of integrating students in this way. Undergraduate student researchers—mentored by faculty members—were trained to moderate student focus groups, administer post-internship surveys, and oversee the collection of photos and narratives from students who completed internships. These student researchers also helped craft focus-group and survey questions, participated in the coding and analysis of data, and presented findings both on campus and at national conferences. In short, students engaged in HIPs (i.e., mentored research) to study HIPs (i.e., internships) are a full-circle moment. Student researchers on the HIPs@the Beach team report several benefits to their participation beyond the ability to hone research skills including an increased sense of confidence, leadership experience, and a deep sense of pride knowing they contributed to efforts that will benefit other first-generation, undergraduate Students of Color like themselves (Lopez et al., 2021).

In the same inclusive vein, we advocate for greater input from site supervisors, not just about their student interns' performance, but also, in a nod to holistic understanding, about their hosting experiences and interactions with the university. Supervisors have a unique perspective on internship quality as they can comment on the match between student and site goals and provide critical input on how internship curriculum and student learning align with industry needs. Site supervisor feedback may be especially helpful for campuses completing internship program reviews, including those using tools like the Internship Scorecard developed by Hora et al. (2020). This tool helps distinguish internship programs based on purpose (format), quality, and equitable access. If we are to invite sites to provide input on our internship programs though, we must be willing to embrace the counternarratives to our stories of internship success (rather than silencing them) as critical feedback could prove useful for improving our internal internship policies and practices (Lange & Stewart, 2019).

Analyzing assessment data

The choices we have and the challenges we encounter when analyzing assessment data matter in an EDIA context. Amassing data should not be the end goal; rather, we have a responsibility to use data to inform targeted program improvements, and, of course, to celebrate the success of our internship programs and student interns. The first analytic step is to disaggregate assessment data by student demographics (social identities) to examine whether certain groups of students benefit more (or in different ways) from their completion of internships and to determine if our internship opportunities are truly equitable for those we strive to serve (an issue of intersequity). When we do not disaggregate our data, we run the risk of masking important variation between groups of students and make it difficult to interpret findings (Kilgo, 2022).

Zilvinskis (2019) provides an example of how informative and compelling disaggregating data can be. In his multi-level modeling of the National Survey of Student Engagement data, he uncovered inconsistencies in the way various HIPs characteristics are related to desired outcomes. For internships, more faculty feedback and real-world application were positively related to higher order learning and student satisfaction, but not so for Black students. His findings suggest that we: "should give pause when trying to create uniform experiences for students, and instead, should consider the ways these experiences should be adjusted to support diverse groups of students" (Zilvinskis, 2019, p. 705).

A challenge to disaggregating assessment data is small sample sizes. It is impossible to compare the internship experiences of Latino and Black students, for example, if your sample does not include sufficient numbers of these students—an issue of statistical power to detect differences (Wilcox et al., 2018). Concerted efforts, thus, must be made to sample (or even oversample) students from minoritized groups to ensure adequate representation. As an alternative to the deconstruction of internships experiences artificially along the lines of single social identities like gender and ethnicity, we propose adopting more holistic person-centered approaches that recognize how the intersectionality of students' multiple identities are related to (or can shape) internship experiences. We posit that we cannot separate race and gender, for example, when looking at a Black woman's internship experiences. We also contend that the various benefits of completing internships are not independent; indeed, there may be combinations of benefits (or challenges) that best characterize or define internship experiences for groups of students and thus warrant a more holistic examination. Further, there may be utility in accessing internships within the context of other high-impact practices. We suspect that there are cumulative effects of participating in multiple high-impact practices, effects we cannot discern unless we examine the sequencing of those high-impact practices.

A project on the California State University, Long Beach campus provides an example of taking a more holistic approach to identifying the benefits of completing internships (Rojas et al., 2021). Data were collected from over 3,500 liberal arts students who completed academic internships between 2015 and 2019. At the end of their internships, students completed a survey that asked about career-related benefits (e.g., networking, development of career-related skills), personal benefits (e.g., learning about one's own strengths and weaknesses, obtaining a greater understanding of diverse points of view), and overall satisfaction with their internship experiences. Instead of examining each category of benefits and overall internship satisfaction separately, we used latent class analysis, an approach that helps uncover hidden groupings or subtypes in data (Weller et al., 2020). Analyses revealed four groups of students, each defined by a unique set or combination of internship benefits. Group 1 represented overall negative experiences where students reported few benefits (career-related or personal) and low satisfaction with their internship experiences. More women and Asian students were in this group. Conversely, Group 2 was an overall positive group where students reported benefits across the board (career-related and personal) and high satisfaction with their internship experiences. There were more men in this group as compared to other groups and fewer Asian students (Rojas et al., 2021).

Perhaps the more interesting groups, and those that best highlight the usefulness of latent class analyses, are the two mixed-experience groups (Rojas et al., 2021). Group 3 included students who reported personal benefits such as learning about their own strengths and weaknesses but did not report high levels of career benefits and reported low satisfaction with their internship site experiences. This group included disproportionately more women, Asian and low-income students. The final group (Group 4) included students who reported high levels of career-related benefits and satisfaction with their internship experiences but low levels of personal benefits. Collectively, these results tell us that for many students, academic internship experiences are not uniformly positive or negative and that to get a more complete picture of how internships benefit students (and to improve our programs), we must examine multiple benefit areas simultaneously (Rojas et al., 2021). Knowing that there are students who experience personal benefits from their academic internships but do not experience any career-related advantages and report low levels of satisfaction with their sites, suggests to us that the academic coursework for these students may be high quality (e.g., offering opportunities for self-reflection) but site placements are lacking. This gives us a place to start as we think about improving our programs to maximize benefits for all students.

Another challenge to analyzing internship assessment data is drawing conclusions about the direction of effects or establishing causal inferences. Zilvinskis (2019) calls attention to the fact that: "It is difficult to declare any causality for opportunities that students are opting into. Do students have higher outcomes because of their participation in HIPs or do students with higher outcomes also choose to participate in these experiences?" (p. 705). This is particularly problematic when attempting to identify the benefits of academic internships, as most students complete internships in their junior or senior years and thus may already possess (prior to doing an internship) the very skills we are hoping to influence. An optimal way to parse out selection biases or pre-internship confounding factors from internship effects would be to employ a control group of students with the same demographic and academic characteristics and skills but who do not complete internships. The use of control groups is itself challenging though as a true control group requires random assignment and it is not feasible (or ethical) to randomly assign students to internship participation (and the control group of non-participants). Analytic techniques such as regression models and the use of propensity score matching represent quasi-control alternatives yet require staff who have expertise in these more advanced analytic methods.

This chapter substantiates a long-standing claim attributed to educator Carol Ann Tomlinson (2014): "Assessment is today's means of modifying tomorrow's instruction" (p. 17). Indeed, we cannot improve our internship programs to ensure equitable access and participation for all students if we do not know which students are currently completing internships and whether (and how) these experiences confer benefits. And the only way to know is through strategic tracking and assessment practices that rely on both quantitative and qualitative methods and center student voices. Once again, we make a nod to the human resource and structural frames of leadership (Bolman & Gallos, 2011) as effective internship assessment will require a commitment on our campuses to resource the people doing the work and infrastructures that support cross-division and unit collaboration to collect, analyze, and use data.

References

Benedict, B. J., & Rust, M. M. (2016). *Internships high-impact practice taxonomy*. IUPUI Scholar Works, Indiana University. https://hdl.handle.net/1805/21506

Bolman, L. G., & Gallos, J. V. (2011). *Reframing academic leadership*. Jossey-Bass.

CSULB University Strategic Communications. (2021). *BEACH 2030: A roadmap for the next decade*. California State University.

Dolan, D. M., Kilbourne, J., Walker, M., & Breaux, G. (2022). High-impact practices and equity: Pathways to student success in general education courses at a large urban community college. In J. Zilvinskis, J. Kinzie, J. Daday, K. O'Donnell, & C. Vande Zande (Eds.), *Delivering on the promise of high-impact practices: Research and models for achieving equity, fidelity, impact, and scale* (pp. 151–163). Stylus.

Finley, A. (2019, November). *A comprehensive approach to assessment of high-impact practices* (Occasional Paper No. 41). University of Illinois and Indiana University, National Institute for Learning Outcomes Assessment. www.learningoutcomesassessment.org/

Finley, A., McNair, T., & Clayton-Pedersen, A. (2022). Designing equity-centered high-impact practices. In J. Zilvinskis, J. Kinzie, J. Daday, K. O'Donnell, & C. Vande Zande (Eds.), *Delivering on the promise of high-impact practices: Research and models for achieving equity, fidelity, impact, and scale* (pp. 17–29). Stylus.

Hora, M. (2022). Internships for all? How inequitable access to internships hinders the promise and potential of high-impact practices and work-based learning. In J.

Zilvinskis, J. Kinzie, J. Daday, K. O'Donnell, & C. Vande Zande (Eds.), *Delivering on the promise of high-impact practices: Research and models for achieving equity, fidelity, impact, and scale* (pp. 113–123). Stylus.

Hora, M. T., Wolfgram, M., Brown, R., Colston, J., Zhang, J., Chen, Z., & Chen, Z. (2020). *The Internship Scorecard: A new framework for evaluating college internships on the basis of purpose, quality and equitable access. Research Brief #11.* Center for Research on College-Workforce Transitions. University of Wisconsin-Madison. https://ccwt.wisc.edu/wp-content/uploads/2022/04/ccwt_report_The-Internship-Scorecard.pdf

Kilgo, C. A. (2022). Methodological challenges of studying high-impact practices for minoritized populations. In J. Zilvinskis, J. Kinzie, J. Daday, K. O'Donnell, & C. Vande Zande (Eds.), *Delivering on the promise of high-impact practices: Research and models for achieving equity, fidelity, impact, and scale* (pp. 40–49). Stylus.

Kinzie, J. (2020). How to reorient assessment and accreditation in the time of COVID-19 disruption. *Assessment Update, 32*(4), 4–5. https://doi.org/10.1002/au.30219

Kinzie, J., McCormick, A. C., Gonyea, R. M., Dugan, B., & Silberstein, S. (2020). *Assessing quality and equity in high-impact practices: Comprehensive report.* Indiana University Center for Postsecondary Research. https://hdl.handle.net/2022/25712quality/index.html

Kinzie, J., McCormick, A. C., Gonyea, R. M., Dugan, B., & Silberstein, S. (2021, March). Getting beyond the label. *Liberal Education, ASCU.* www.aacu.org/liberaleducation/articles/-on-quality-in-label-three-takes-on-quality-in-high-impact-practices.

Kinzie, J., Silberstein, S., McCormick A. C., Gonyea, R. M., & Dugan, B. (2021), Centering racially minoritized student voices in high-impact practices. *Change: The Magazine of Higher Learning, 53*(4), 6–14. https://doi.org/10.1080/00091383.2021.1930976

Lange, A., & Stewart, D.-L. (2019). High-impact practices. In E. S. Abes, S. R. Jones, & D.-L. Stewart (Eds.), *Rethinking college student development theory using critical frameworks* (1st ed., pp. 221–236). Stylus.

Lopez, C., Kelly, K. R., Maloles, C., Nolasco, C., & Manke, B. (2021, October 24–27). *Using HIPs to study HIPs: Designing and implementing a student-centered and student-led assessment project.* Paper presentation, Assessment Institute Annual Meeting.

Morales, C., Neves, S., Mokatish, S., Maloles, C., Min, V., George, N., & Kelly, K. (2022, April 27–May 1). *High-impact practices: Investigating the impact of internship participation during COVID-19 on student cognitive and psychosocial outcomes.* Poster presentation, Western Psychological Association Annual Convention, Portland, OR.

National Survey of College Internships. (2023). *What is the NSCI?* www.collegeinternshipsurvey.org/

O'Shea, J., Hoover, M., & Hunt, J. (2022). Increasing student access and learning in employment and internship experiences. In J. Zilvinskis, J. Kinzie, J. Daday, K. O'Donnell, & C. Vande Zande (Eds.), *Delivering on the promise of high-impact practices: Research and models for achieving equity, fidelity, impact, and scale* (pp. 188–198). Stylus.

Rojas, L., Stormes, K., Manke, B., & Ocular, G. (2021, May 14). *Assessing internships: For whom and under what circumstances are academic internships a high-impact practice?* Poster presentation, CSULB Data Fellows Annual Symposium, Long Beach, CA.

Shippensburg University. (2023). *Non credit internships.* https://career.ship.edu/channels/non-credit-internships/

Strada Education Foundation. (2023). *Who we are.* https://stradaeducation.org/who-we-are/

Tomlinson, C. (2014). *The differentiated classroom: Responding to the needs of all learners* (2nd ed.). Association for Supervision and Curriculum Development.

Valentine, J., & Price, D. (2021). *Scaling high-impact practices to improve community college student outcomes: Evidence from the Tennessee Board of Regents.* Lumina Foundation. https://files.eric.ed.gov/fulltext/ED611261.pdf

Wang, C., & Burris, M. A. (1997). Photovoice: Concept, methodology, and use for participatory needs assessment. *Health Education Behavior, 24*(3), 369–387. https://doi.org/10.1177/109019819702400309

Weller, B. E., Bowen, N. K., & Faubert, S. J. (2020). Latent class analysis: A Guide to best practice. *Journal of Black Psychology, 46*(4), 287–311. https://doi.org/10.1177/0095798420930932

Wilcox, R., Peterson T. J., & McNitt-Gray, J. L. (2018). Data analyses when sample sizes are small: Modern advances for dealing with outliers, skewed distributions, and heteroscedasticity. *Journal of Applied Biomechanics, 34*(4), 258–261. https://doi.org/10.1123/jab.2017-0269

Worthen, M. (2018, February 23). The misguided drive to measure learning outcomes. *New York Times. Opinion.* nytimes.com

Yosso, T. J. (2005). Whose culture has capital? A critical race theory discussion of community cultural wealth. *Race Ethnicity and Education, 8*(1), 69–91. https://doi.org/10.1080/1361332052000341006

Young, K., Kelly, K., Lopez, C., Trimble, B., & Manke, B. (2022, April 21). *High-impact practices at CSULB: How (and for whom) do they promote student success.* Paper presentation, CSULB Provosts' Timely Graduation Symposium, Long Beach, CA.

Yousey-Elsener, K., & Pagan, K. (2022). Using assessment data to expand access to high-impact practices for every student. In J. Zilvinskis, J. Kinzie, J. Daday, K. O'Donnell, & C. Vande Zande (Eds.), *Delivering on the promise of high-impact practices: Research and models for achieving equity, fidelity, impact, and scale* (pp. 209–218). Stylus.

Zilvinskis, J. (2019). Measuring quality in high-impact practices. *Higher Education, 78*, 687–709. https//doi.org/10.1007/s10734-019-00365-9

Zilvinskis, J., Kinzie, J., Daday, J., O'Donnell, K., & Vande Zande, C. (2022). *Delivering on the promise of high-impact practices: Research and models for achieving equity, fidelity, impact, and scale.* Stylus.

Afterword

Beyond *InternsHIPs*

Despite the issues facing today's internship system, including many of the fraught topics broached throughout this book—ethics, fairness, compensation, and student equity—we echo Perlin's sentiments that "There is still time to get internships right" (2012, p. 202). So, how does atonement begin? Our experience suggests at the micro-level and strategically. Gather just a few internship enthusiasts/ champions who are open to critical dialogue, and trust in time because

> People tend to notice transformation once it has already happened, and often get the impression that because it became big that it started that way. That's almost never true. Initiatives become transformative through building success upon success. You do not need to convince everybody all at once. You need to start with a small group that's enthusiastic about change
> (Satell, 2023, p. 6)

The key is to embrace provocative praxis at every turn while engaging your leadership frames. Although change, particularly in university settings, happens at a glacial pace, you must be ready for opportunities to dialogue whenever they present themselves—from a department meeting with colleagues to a chance encounter with the university president in an elevator—as the big changes are the imperceptible accumulation of small ones. By recognizing this enigmatic phenomenon, we find comfort in the oxymoronic phrase, "patient sense of urgency," which, on the one hand, implies tolerance for the uncontrollable, and on the other, to be able to advocate fiercely on demand.

Once we find our people—it is crucial to be in conversation with a range of stakeholders including faculty, staff, students, and internship partners, as one person cannot engage or be engaged in isolation—explaining and validating provocative praxis as part of the rules of engagement as a first order of business gives everyone permission to feel vulnerable and uneasy. Welcome these feelings. Normalize them. Although provocative praxis may run counter to Freud's pleasure principle, superficial bandages on deep wounds only fester. To use another medical metaphor, provocative praxis identifies the root cause rather than merely addressing proximal causes. As a consensus builds that something has to be done, direct the momentum toward action. Engaging in provocative praxis conversations sets the stage for the next steps to begin to lead by example. In fact, provocative praxis led to the establishment of a new Academic Internships Office at California State University, Long Beach (2023) to address inequalities in students' access to and participation in high-impact internships and to develop institutional infrastructure to support, sustain, and scale academic internship programs across campus.

Although this book intentionally targets internships as a high-impact practice, its gleanings are applicable beyond higher education. Indeed, once we begin to engage in and subscribe to the art of provocative praxis, we more easily see how it applies to—if not drives—almost any (leadership) context. Curators and conservators at New York's Museum of Modern Art, for example, have commented on the benefits of working together on a current exhibition of Georia O'Keefe's paintings. They note, in a nod to the previous paragraph, "It takes time to see, but we always see more when we look together" (Neufeld & Friedman, 2023). Indeed, the collaborative work between the curator and the paper conservator to analyze the O'Keefe drawings and watercolors exemplifies key components of provocative praxis: the importance of being in discussion with others ("seeing more when we look together") and the value of engaging in conversation with others with differing perspectives (that of a paper conservator and a curator, respectively). The spark generated from provocation affords an opportunity to challenge each other's ideas and our own.

Throughout our book, we exemplify in implicit and explicit ways why provocative praxis must anticipate the implementation of any internship program in the twenty-first century. Provocative praxis shuns prescriptive rigidity and instead embraces design and futurist thinking. This process, by definition, is campus-specific, collaborative and demands that stakeholders engage fearlessly and strategically. Anyone who champions phrases such as "student readiness" and "inclusive excellence" is, in fact, closer to provocative praxis than they may think, as it brings to fruition those phrases in actionable—as opposed to performative—ways. Moreover, the more we engage in provocative praxis, the more we realize that it is not adjacent to but rather at the heart of authentic student success. As such, it becomes relevant to other HIPs with boundless applicability. Ultimately, provocative praxis becomes much more than a critical tool to probe internship equity; it is a beacon for and harbinger of all leadership endeavors in and beyond the academy.

References

Neufeld, L., & Friedman, S. (2023, April 4). Georgia O'Keefe leaves a paper trail. *MOMA Magazine*. www.moma.org/magazine/articles/870.

Perlin, R. (2012). *Intern nation: How to earn nothing and learn little in the brave new economy*. Verso.

Satell, G. (2023). To implement change, you don't need to convince everyone at once. *Harvard Business Review*, 1–7. hbr.org

Index

academic affairs: faculty focus in 29; student and 30–32
access: campus policies/procedures and 36–38; of EDIA 6, 9; equitable student, to internships 18–21, 49–50; funding and, to internships 33–36; to HIPs 1–3; Students of Color and 41–45
Advancing Inclusive Mentoring (AIM) Program 78
Alderman, B. 77
American Association of Colleges and Universities (AACU) 33; Institute on High-Impact Practices and Student Success 33
American Institute of Architects 79
Amherst College Charles Hamilton Houston Internship Program 55
apprenticeships 56–57
Arcelus, V. J. 29
Arizona State University 82
Arthius, J. 57
Assessing Quality and Equity in High-Impact Practices project 93
assessment of equity-centered HIPS 89–103; analyzing assessment data 100–103; latent class analyses 102–103; identifying who will do work of 98–100; overview of 89; starting point for 89–92; student internship experiences and 92–98; student voices and 100
asset mapping 91–92
Association of Public and Land-grant Universities 64
authentic partnerships *see* partnerships
autonomy 72–73
Aviate Academy 82

Baker, V. L. 47
Ball, S. J. 9
bandwidth 43
Bandwidth Recovery: Helping Students Reclaim Cognitive Resources Lost to Poverty, Racism and Social Marginalization (Verschelden) 42–43
Beach 2030 strategic plan, CSULB 19, 90
Bensimon, E. M. 9, 10
Berkeley Beacon 50
Best Value Colleges 19
Big Picture Issues (BPIs) 13
Binghamton University High-Impact Practices Innovations Council (HIPIC) 98–99
Black Lives Matter 1, 45
Blackmore, J. 5
Bolman, L. G. 12–13, 18, 25
Bowman, C. G. 53
breaking frame 13
Brookings Institution 1
Busteed, B. 81–82

calculated voluntarism 49
California Competes 63, 64
California Dream Act students 35
California Intern Network 82
Californians for All College Corps Program 35
California State University, Long Beach 18, 55, 89; Academic Internships Office 90, 98; Advancing Inclusive Mentoring (AIM) Program 78; Beach 2030 strategic plan 19, 90; CalState S4 91; College Corps program 67; discipline- and

major-specific internship courses 48; Long Beach Community Internship Project 40–41
campus policies/procedures, institutional infrastructure and 36–38
Career Path Internship Program (CPIP) 18–19, 27
career readiness 64
Casciaro, T. 29, 31–32
CEE Centre For Young Black Professionals 82
Center for Career Engagement & Opportunity (CEO) 55–56
Center for Research on College-Workforce Transitions (CCWT) 94–95
centralization: community organization host sites for 23–24; institutional infrastructure and 22–25, 64; for internships 23–24; partial 22; risk/liability management and 22–23; transparency and 24
Cerdin, J. L. 56, 57
Chadwick, R. 4
Charitybuzz 52
Chepp, V. 10
Cho, C. S. 71
Clemson University On-Campus Internship program 56
coalitions, institutional infrastructure and 28–33
collaborations: cultural brokering and 31–32; defined 28; institutional infrastructure and 28–33; organization relationships and 33
College Corps@the Beach 57–58, 67
College of Science at Swansea University 80–81
Collins, M. 51
common cause 30
Commonwealth Care Alliance 65, 66
Community College of Baltimore County HIPS Infusion Steering Committee 99
community cultural wealth model 11, 74, 94
community organizations 62–85; authentic partnerships with 62–68; benefits to partnering, and supervisors 84–85; as host sites for centralization 23–24; internship programs beyond university 82–84; overview of 62; partners as supervisors 68–70; partners' roles in curriculum 80–82; site supervisors, training 70–80; *see also* partnerships
Conflict Transformation 20–21
Connecticut College, College Internship Program 55
Crawford, P. 64
Crenshaw, K. 45
crisis 1
critical gaps 1–2
critical terms in internships 9–12
CSULB *see* California State University, Long Beach
cultural broker 31–32
cultural capital 43, 48
cultural competency 71, 73
culture, defined 43
curriculum 7, 46, 80–82

Dallas Cowboys 82
deficit thinking 11
Delivering on the Promise of High-Impact Practices: Research and Models for Achieving Equity, Fidelity, Impact and Scale (Zilvinkis) 89
design team 47
design thinking 21–22
discomfort 3–4
discrimination 73, 94
Disney World internship program 11–12
diversity 9; training 73–74
Diversity, Equity & Inclusion Internship Program 83
Doyle, A. 41
Dream Hoarders (Reeves) 6
dream hoarding 54
Drew, K. 52
Durack, K. T. 52

EDIA (equity, diversity, inclusion, and access) 6, 9
Edwards, K. A. 54
80 Million Strong 54
Elements of Effective Practice for Mentoring (Garringer) 79
engaged inclusivity 43
Ensher, E. A. 76

Index 111

Ensuring Quality & Taking High-Impact Practices to Scale (Kuh and O'Donnel) 2–3
equity 5, 9, 45; in classroom 46–49; defined 9–10; leading with 9; unpaid internships and 49–58; whitewashing of 10
equity-mindedness 43
European Mentoring and Coaching Council 79
Experiential Learning Cycle 11; phases of 11

faculty developers 47
faculty/staff workload: institutional infrastructure and 25–28; unpaid internships and 26–27; women *vs.* men in 25–27
Fair Labor Standards Act (FSLA) 6, 10, 22
Finely, A. 27, 38, 89
Fink, W. 64
Finley, A. 1–2, 48, 89–90, 91, 92, 95
Fisher, F. 48
Florida State University 36, 56; Internship Council 99
Foucault, M. 3
Four I's: HIPs and 3; unpaid internships and 66
frame break 13
funding, institutional infrastructure and 33–36

gadfly 21
Gallos, J. V. 12–13, 18, 25
Gandhi, M. 71
Gardener, P. 51
Giles, M. 64, 67
Gray, K. 55–56
Gregersen, H. 4
Griffin, K. A. 47

Harvard University Director's Internship Program 55
Hatch, D. K. 3
Hatton, E. 25
Henkel 82
Hernandez, C. 66
higher education 20, 28, 30, 63, 64, 79, 80, 89, 107
High-Impact Educational Practices: What They Are, Who Has Access to Them, and Why They Matter (Kuh) 2
high-impact practices (HIPs) 1–4; assessment of 89–103; as concept 3; crises and 1–2; discomfort and 3–4; Four I's and 3
High-Impact Practices in Online Education: Research and Best Practices (Linder & Mattison Hayes) 6
HIPs *see* high-impact practices (HIPs)
HIPs Quality Assessment Tool 93–94, 96; Students of Color application of 93–94
HIPS@the Beach 89, 95–98, 100; Photovoice and 96–98
Hora, M. 40, 41, 42, 49–50, 52, 70, 73, 89, 94, 100
"How Internships Replaced the Entry-Level Job" (Waxman) 6
Hughes, A. M. 79
human resources leadership frame 12

Idaho State University 18; Career Path Internship Program 18–19, 27, 32–34, 56; paid internships 33–34
inclusion 9
Indiana University Center for Postsecondary Research 93
Indigenous Land rights movement 1
INROADS 82
Insight into Diversity 49
institutional infrastructure 18–38; campus policies/procedures and 36–38; centralization and 22–25, 64; collaborations/coalitions and 28–33; faculty/staff workload and 25–28; funding and 33–36; overview of 18; strong senior leadership and 18–22
intern abuse 11
Intern Bridge 51
intern ready status 66
internships: applicable credit/accompanying coursework debate regarding 47–48; centralized risk management for 22–24; crises and 2; critical gaps and 1–2; critical terms in 9–12; faculty/staff workload

and 25–28; feminization of 14, 26–27; history and evolution of 6–8; Kuh and 2–3; labelling of 91; parasitic 11–12; programs beyond university 82–84; provocative praxis and 4–6; *see also* institutional infrastructure
Internships, Service Learning, and Volunteering Abroad: Successful Models and Best Practices (Nolting) 5–6
intersectionality 9, 10; defined 45; Students of Color 40–41
intersequity 10, 45–46, 53
inventory taking 91–92

Jahsman, E. 18
Johnson, M. 71

Kennedy, John F. 1
Kessel, S. 46
Kids Sports News Network (KSSN) 64, 67
Kinzie, J. 8, 42, 48, 89, 92, 94, 98
Kuh, G. D. 2–3, 7, 8, 45, 48
Kupersmidt, J. 69

Langan-Riekhof, M. 1
leadership frames: centralizing internship tasks and 25; described 12–13; human resources 12; political 12; structural 12; symbolic 12
LePeau, L. 21
Li, M. 76, 84
liability 22, 25, 38, 39, 46, 47, 72
linguistic racism 73
Lipp, M. 53
Lo, T. 51
Long Beach Community Internship Project (LBCIP) 40–41, 57
Lopes, B. 65, 68
Lord, T. 14
Luedke, C. L. 74, 75, 76
Lumina Foundation 93

McCormick, A. C. 48, 92
McCoy, D. L. 75
McHugh, P. P. 68, 70
McNair, T. 1–2
McNair, T. B. 43, 46
memos of understanding (MOUs) 22–23, 24
mental bandwidth 43

mental health 50
Mental Health First Aid 28
MENTOR 79
Mentoring Essentials (American Institute of Architects) 79
mentors/mentoring: challenges and 70; characteristics 71; partners and 68–70; site supervisor training and 70–80; supervisor support and 69–70
#MeToo 1
Michigan Founders Fund (MFF) 83–84
microaggressions 73, 94
Mitrano-Meda, S. 71
Museus, S. D. 11
mutualism 12
Myers, S. 28

National Association of College and Employers (NACE) 8, 49, 51, 65; Internship and Co-Op Report 84
National Association of Student Personnel Administrators (NASPA) 30, 33
National Council of Architectural Registration Board (NCARB) 79
National Institute for Learning Outcomes Assessment 2
National Survey of College Internships (NSCI) 94–95
National Survey of Student Engagement (NSSE) 93, 101
navigational capital 42
New College of Florida 55
non-interns 40
Norman, J. 50

O'Donnel, K. 2–3
O'Halloran, K. C. 29
O'Keeffe, G. 107
O'Neill, N. 47–49
O'Shea J. 99
outreach 23, 24, 25, 27, 33, 55

Pagan, K. 99
parasitism 11–12
partnerships: authentic, with community organizations 62–68; barriers to 63–64; career readiness and 64; educational curriculum and 80–82; geographical

context and 65; organizations and supervisors, predatory 67; benefits to 84–85; as supervisors 68–70
Partners in Learning (PALS) 77–78
Peretti, J.-M. 56, 57
Perlin, R. 2, 7, 8, 11–12, 15, 40, 49, 50–51, 52–54, 56
Peterson, D. 55–56
Photovoice 96–98
Pisano, G. P. 22, 30
political leadership frame 12
Political Science Internships: Towards Best Practices (American Political Science Association) 5
Powell, K. 14
provocative, defined 4
provocative praxis 4–6, 9, 106–107; equity and 45; safe spaces for 20–21; *see also* community organizations

Realities: A Collection of Short Stories (Lo) 51
Reeves, M. 84
Reeves, R. 6, 54
reframing 13
resistance capital 94
risk 22–25, 33, 47, 90
risk management 22, 44, 64
Roberts, L.J. 81
Rojas, L. 101–102
role model 69, 74–75
Rossi-Le, L. 80
Rothschild, C. L. 50
Rothschild, P. C. 50

Sarasota-Manatee Arts & Humanities (SMAH) Internship Program 55
scaffolding 41, 43, 72, 78
senior leadership: accountability and 19; institutional infrastructure and 18–22; strong, in internship landscape 19; transparency and 19
sensemaking 46
Shearer, J. 65
Shippensburg University 91
Silberstein, S. 42, 94
silos 29–30, 31, 46, 85
site supervisor training 70–80; content of 71; cultural competency/diversity training 73–76;

delivery and mode of 76–78; online materials for 79; overview of 70–71; prior mentoring experience and 71; program requirements and 72; student expectations and 72; task autonomy and 72–73
Smith College Praxis Program 55
social gadflies 21
social justice 7, 10, 34, 49
State Farm 82
Steinmetz, K. 45
St-Jean, É. 71
Strada Education Network 94
strategic plan 19, 30, 38
structural leadership frame 12, 19, 25, 32, 38, 53, 57, 84, 103
student affairs 7, 28–33, 98
student internship experiences, assessment of 92–98
Student Loan Hero 49
Student Opportunity Center 91
Student Placement Agreements 22, 23
Students of Color 10, 41–45; internships 44, 83; intersectionality 40–41; parasitic internships and 12; social capital 43–44; supervisory relationships and 74–76
Student Success in College: Creating Conditions That Matter (Kuh) 7
supervisors: and organizations, benefits to partnering 84–85; partnerships as 68–70; Students of Color and 74–76; support 69–70; training of 70–80
symbolic leadership frame 12

task autonomy 72–73
teamwork 12, 30, 47
Tennessee Board of Regents 99
Thijssen, F. S. L. 46
This is What I know About Art (Drew) 52
Thrive and Shine LLC 83
Tomlinson, C. A. 103
Tu, M. 76, 84

Ultimate Guide to Internships: 100 Steps to Get a Great Internship and Thrive in It, The (Woodard) 6
United Airlines 82
United Negro College Fund 1
University Enterprises, Inc. 82

114 Index

University of Canberra 77
University of Dreams 54
University of North Texas 82
University of Wisconsin Center for Research on College-Workforce Transitions (CCWT) 94–95
unmet financial need 37
unpaid internships 26–27; apprenticeships and 56–57; creative internship funding ideas 55–56; dream hoarding and 54; as equity crime 49–58; federal funding for 54; Four I's and 66; Hora on 49–50, 52; intersequity issues 53; Lo fictional intern examples of 51; NACE position on 49, 51; Perlin on 50–54; psychosocial effects of 50; student salary/employment outcomes and 51; Students of Color and 53

Vailas, A. 19
Van Tine, T. 83
Verschelden, C. 42–43
virtual internships 65–66

Waxman, O. B. 6–7
Well-Suited 66
Well-Suited Club House 66
Westwind School of Aeronautics 82
whiteness 10, 48
white privilege 6
William and Mary 19
Willison, S. 84
Wolfgram, M. 70, 73

Yosso, T. J. 11, 41, 42, 43, 48, 74, 90, 94
Young, K. A. 77, 78, 96
Yousey-Elsener, K. 99

Zhang, T. 85
Zilvinskis, J. 3, 89, 101, 102

For Product Safety Concerns and Information please contact our EU representative GPSR@taylorandfrancis.com
Taylor & Francis Verlag GmbH, Kaufingerstraße 24, 80331 München, Germany

www.ingramcontent.com/pod-product-compliance
Lightning Source LLC
Chambersburg PA
CBHW051754230426
43670CB00012B/2280